ART: MAGIC, IMPULSE, AND CONTROL

ART: MAGIC, IMPULSE, AND CONTROL

A Guide to Viewing

by WILLIAM BRADLEY

Prentice-Hall, Inc., *Englewood Cliffs, New Jersey*

701
N71
.B69

Library of Congress Cataloging in Publication Data

Bradley, William, 1934–
    Art: magic, impulse, and control.

    Includes bibliograhical references.
    1. Art—Psychology.   2. Visual perception.
    I. Title.
    N71.B69   701   72–8963
    ISBN   0-13-046664-6
    ISBN   0-13-046656-5 (pbk.)

10 9 8 7 6 5 4 3 2 1

Prentice-Hall International, Inc., *London*
Prentice-Hall of Australia, Pty. Ltd., *Sydney*
Prentice-Hall of Canada, Ltd., *Toronto*
Prentice-Hall of India Private Limited, *New Delhi*
Prentice-Hall of Japan, Inc., *Tokyo*

About the author: Little is known about William Bradley,
Associate Professor of Art Education,
The Pennsylvania State University.

CONTENTS

PREFACE, ix

INTRODUCTION, 1

MAGIC, IMPULSE, AND CONTROL, 5

SOME HISTORIC AND CONTEMPORARY EXAMPLES, 20

MATERIALS, TOOLS, AND PROCESSES, 53
Drawing, 54
Sculpture, 7 2
Painting, 9 4
Graphics, 103
Architecture, 129
The Functional and Decorative Arts, 151

THE ARTIST, 166

INDEX, 180

PREFACE

It is a very difficult task to make material alive and meaningful for use in large introductory courses, partly because so many areas of complex content are touched upon without adequate explication, and partly because of a student mind-set against compulsory courses and especially in areas outside their professional interests. The material in this book was developed as adjunct material to a fully fledged introductory text during several terms of teaching large classes in the Universities of Minnesota, Wisconsin, and particularly, Maryland. In these classes, a typical lecture was conducted in the dark in an amphitheatre setting. With the neck microphone, pointer, and notes I moved quickly over the material to be covered (or uncovered) for the course. My projectionist and assistants were invaluable to the smooth operation of the class machine. But the missing ingredient appeared to be empathy in this setting. Student interest in the arts often hung in the balance. Examinations, anonymous notes, and amnesty pleas all pointed to the need for a more viable pedagogy.

At the University of Maryland, our solution was to establish groups which met with the teaching assistant to discuss the content and implications of the lectures and we soon discovered that, for the most part, the lectures dealt too severely with historiographic models and that the sentient dimensions required for personal meaning were absent. It seemed most fruitful to discuss models or ways of viewing art which hopefully lead to the development of other, more private meaningful views of the world of art and artists.

The second discovery was that a careful explication of terms including processes and materials and the effect these have on the artistic outcome could not be adequately handled during class time without impinging upon other more important considerations. It was clear that an inexpensive handbook was needed which could become a part of each student's personal library; one which carefully described the major processes in all the visual arts through graphic illustration and description.

This work is, therefore, a supplemental ingredient in what was considered to be a more acceptable format for the course: the lectures which dealt with an overview of the arts in history combined with small discussion groups, and a handbook which described briefly one typology for viewing art. Hopefully such a typology could lead to model building discussions in the small groups along with an expanded discussion of the materials, tools, and processes used in producing art and a look at the artist, himself, as a particular functionary in society and culture.

Its success for me and my students was immediately apparent and it is for this reason that it is herein compiled for wider distribution. Its use is by no means limited to a supplemental one but may include a wide variety of courses where an introductory view of the visual arts, a concise description of processes and materials in the visual arts, and a look at the artist himself is appropriate.

William Bradley
University Park, Pennsylvania

INTRODUCTION

How do we perceive works of art? What is there about these objects, movements, sounds, and words which continues to be a source for both scholarly and emotional debate? What is a work of art? What does it say to us? These questions often represent an honest desire to understand our relationship to the arts in this complex time and, secondly, they reflect a tenacious attraction to the singular or particular experience that the arts provide. The questions are certainly not intrusive. They are honestly born out of a natural and human inquisitiveness. There have been times in our history, however, when these questions would not have had the same meaning and would, perhaps, have been inappropriate, for art was (in those times) related to specific spiritual functions: objects were made, songs were sung, and dances were performed for specific purposes. In the case of the visual arts, works were often destroyed or discarded after their intended function was fulfilled. To ask how we perceive such works would be to acknowledge that we did not belong to the group, for works of art were made not so much for viewing as for using.

In our present-day world there are certain primitive populations who continue to use art in this way, but in our complex, developed society we have expanded the functions to which the arts relate. The visual arts, music, dance, theatre, and writing are often seen as historical record, group expression, means of problem solving, and commodity—as well as personal expression. With all of these approaches to the study of the arts there is ample reason for contemporary man to ask such questions. They can be serious attempts to penetrate the various modes of inquiry which appear to exist in a complex society.

Art is a record peculiar to its time, and among all records (including written ones) the visual and aural arts continue to serve as primary touchstones for the interpretation of meanings and values indigenous to past civilizations. Art is also born in the mind and hands of the artist who lives within (although sometimes at the periphery) of a social group, so that his expressions are often group expressions as well, pointing to the values and styles of the culture from which they spring.

The process of making art is a "way of knowing" which often rejects empirical and logical inquiry in favor of sentience and immediate perceptions. It is a problem-solving behavior which demands that the problem itself be discovered and then solved. This dimension is one of the most intriguing and puzzling, for prior knowledge and procedure are only tangentially related to this process.

Today, art is bought and sold like cheese. It is often found in its most pedestrian forms in dime stores, airport terminals, and sidewalk festivals, but it is also found at levels reaching to the market for authentic and profound material. The market for the pedestrian in music, theatre, dance, and writing is also very large. Some view the commodity dimension of art as an indication of widespread interest in the arts, inasmuch as the number of people actively engaged in local arts groups and the number of groups outside the arts who are using the arts for expressive purposes have steadily increased; but others see this phenomenon as leisure activity which is honest neither as personal encounter nor as art study. The objects produced by these attempts are directly tied to the models of forming produced in mass education—which in some way seems to be encouraging the sale and production of a particular kind of object.

If our neolithic forefathers could see what we do to our art objects, they would probably be very perplexed. They might wonder why we have museums and galleries for the storage and veneration of objects out of context. They might wonder why we sit and watch dancers perform high art instead of participating in the performance ourselves, or why we sit and listen to a performance of music written several centuries before our time (or even by the people of another culture).

Conversely, contemporary man is often perplexed by the fact that the art fashioned by primitive artists for their society is often ceremoniously destroyed or eventually discarded—that objects intended for specific functions in these groups, such as rituals and celebrations, are treated with impunity after fulfilling their intent or, in some instances, failing to serve it.

We shall explore not only these aspects of both primitive and contemporary art as they relate to magic, belief, and power, but also other aspects of art, which appear to be transcultural, having to do with intention or impulse in art, and control or competence in the producton of art. We shall attempt to look closely at both the formal and informal descriptions of art, and also at the motivations of the artist himself, since some knowledge of the maker may be useful in describing what was made. What we hope to develop is one model by which we can view most (if not all) art objects and art ideas. But we must remember that such a typology is tentative, subject to redefinition when it no longer serves our purposes.

There are many definitions of art and many models for viewing it. Some are brilliantly executed and some are simple. All of them, perhaps, suffer in one way or another, by being either too specific or not specific enough. The problem seems to lie in the nature of definitions themselves. We would not be satisfied without some defi-

three

nition of art, nor would we be satisfied with a complete in-depth definition, since one of the strengths of an individual work of art is its ability to transcend all definitions and live in undefined experience. When we analyze a work of art we are able to ascertain selected surface characteristics which seem to be responsible for the expressive relationships within the work, but our descriptions, by their dissecting nature, do not seem to be effective in isolating that quality of wholeness which makes the work uniquely expressive. In fact, definitions are attempts to simplify highly complex phenomena into something more easily understood. When we define, we necessarily eliminate those aspects which we determine to be less important. There are no quarantees that we aren't eliminating very important aspects of the phenomena when we do this. We should be cautious, therefore, with our acceptance of definitions since, it will always be possible to redefine and rearrange our data.

Still, definitions can provide a model which may lead us to a position of perceptual strength on our way to a fuller enjoyment of works of art. It is much like the adage about leading a horse to water. The personal appreciation of a work of art has to do with being in a perceptual position to relate the work of art to our own experience. Our purpose here will be to discuss certain aspects which go into the quality of the parts as well as the whole, while keeping in mind that extended exposure to works of art and a willingness to forego preconceptions about art are equally important— or perhaps more important—to our understanding and enjoyment of them. We also begin by acknowledging that much of art is as dry as the Sahara for the layman and that, even after the construction of a model definition, our personal likes and dislikes will ultimately determine which aspects of art and which objects we will enjoy.

Most definitions of art stress the extrapersonal or social dimensions of the work, the artist's personal expressiveness, and his production competence. In our definition these three areas are referred to as *magic, impulse,* and *control.*

MAGIC, IMPULSE, AND CONTROL

Art As Magic

There is some evidence that, in man's approximately 1 million years' tenure on earth, belief or faith in his ability to control, in some way, unknown forces which have affected his life has been an integral part of his art production. Power, control, or influence over those aspects of life which directly affect existence has motivated man to produce visual expressions that communicate the most inarticulate of these feelings—which are often by definition the most profound. In primitive art (not to be construed as "bad" or "amateurish" art, but rather as "functional art produced in tribal societies") the extrapersonal aspect of art was by far the most important, since the art was ceremonial. It was not primarily intended for viewing but more often for touching, carrying, wearing, etc. In our society we maintain certain vestiges of extrapersonal art which can be characterized as social symbols—e.g., flags, official symbols (such as the seal of the president), and religious objects. The validity of such objects is often dependent upon group consent, and they are often subject to destruction if they do not serve their intended function. But we also maintain more complex, less well understood archetypes which relate to the perpetual conditions under which men live and die. We still speak to the issues of birth, life, puberty, celebration, ceremony, fear, and death, even though the form of the mythical interpretation related to these events change as societies change. The myths seem to continue in new forms. The "magic" of the new forms in music, dance, theatre, literature, drama, and the visual arts may occur when the form-and-content relationship is capable of touching a particular social group consciousness. We may, perhaps, view the tribal belief in magical forms as having complex parallels in our society as well. First of all, the word *magic* belongs to the history of art. It reminds us of our dark ancestry. The ceremonial "laying on of hands," where hand-fashioned objects were effused with intermediary powers to allay threats, to help in hunting, to increase fertility, and to provide a spiritual dimension to neolithic lives, provided these groups with humanizing, nonsurvival-related, and sometimes aesthetic dimensions. Secondly, magic belongs to the metalanguage—the language beyond spoken or written ones—of territorial groups. All groups maintain amulet and effigylike objects which communicate group feelings without verbalization. Counterculture youth have continued this tradition in their use of buttons, pins, flags, posters, and clothing which, however pedestrian these objects may seem, are at best identified with a spirit and, consequently, an occultlike influence over ideas and other forces. Thirdly, *magic* as a word may be used to describe one dimension of the art experience, since the prefixes magni- and magi- refer to situations or things which are larger than the unit (hence "magnification" and "magician"). The word *magic*—like such other words as *spirit, love, vision, dream,* and *specter*—is symbolic of forces larger than the unit and is effused with energy which makes "electrical" contact possible between us without articulated definitions. We must keep the word, to stand off inundation by the poor promise of knowledge about art. "Knowledge," as one astute observer noted, "keeps no better than fish"; or, to employ another analogy, it requires constant recycling into performance if it is to survive at all. Once we *know* what it is that we felt, we are less apt to *feel* it again. An emotion ceases to be an emotion as soon as we form a clear and distinct idea of it. The nonverbal or inarticulate aspects of communication are partially "felt" or "emotional," and as such derive their very life from the fact that they cannot be explained away.

All art, abstract or not, is clearly subject to degeneration and maudlin imitation if it does not maintain its lifelines to the vital sources of renewal—the human impulses toward the control of survival, knowledge, and vitality.

Because nature is always more natural than art and because art may be described perhaps as being more supernatural than nature, we might view the human social input into art as representative of those mysteries and impulses characteristic of the universal human myths about the unknown and the little-understood. In this way the human involvement in ceremony and celebration, which if often made manifest in expressions of love, joy, hate, anger, incredulity, and faith, may become basic reifications (in the arts) of these relatively constant myths. While it is true that the form of these expressions continues to change as societies and ideas change, the content derived from myths themselves seems relatively constant. Herbert Read discusses this idea as it seems to parallel the other arts, e.g., literature:

> The characters of Shakespeare's great plays are not merely individual characters, for all their realism and fidelity to life, but also prototypes of the passions and aspirations of humanity in general. . . . We may conclude therefore [regarding art], that besides purely formal values . . . there may be psychological values—the values arising out of our common human sympathies and interests, and even those arising out of our subconscious life.[1]

The use of objects intended to perform intergroup functions is often politically based—for influencing or controlling groups as totemic reminders of power, heroism, sources, etc.—as we can often see in state architecture and the officially sanctioned arts of oppressive governments. But subtle and equally proselytizing in intent is the appeal to humor, ridicule, satire, or praise, etc., in works of art which serve as influencing reminders of certain conditional aspects of men's lives. The social commentary of Daumier, Rouault, Goya, and Tooker (and in a more pedestrian way, of Al Capp) are examples of this kind of totemic involvement through subject matter.

But subject matter alone is often insufficient to achieve the feeling required to influence groups or to help groups sense a vicarious control over situations. More often, magic occurs when media, control, and personal interpretations penetrate into group consciousness through various means. Then art becomes a totemic means of understanding and control.

In our earliest records of man's visual expressions (Paleolithic: 27,000–15,000 B.C.), we may speculate, a concern for influence over environment and vital life forces was a strong motivation. His effigies of bison, deer, and tigers seem to indicate a belief that his visual representations helped him to exercise influence over his environment and productivity. His amulets, made to be carried or worn, provide evidence of this same belief (see Fig. 1). Contemporary aborigines apparently maintain a similar need:

> Among the Australian aborigines—who remain today at the level of the early Stone Age hunters—rock paintings depicting plants and animals are, every year, not repainted but touched up, so that new, powerful souls may go out from them and take on new bodies.
> Thus early man, the hunter, believed that in a spiritual manner, through art, he could intervene in the productive processes of nature and influence them in a way favorable to himself.[2]

There is also some evidence to suggest that later civilizations (including our own) have maintained peculiar attachments to this totemic need in their individual and group lives. One possible example is the constant use and development of portraiture in art. It is generally assumed that the macabre neolithic practice of beheading the dead and plastering the skull in order to retain the spirit inside represents the earliest beginning of the art of portraiture. In more advanced dynastic Egypt, the heads of corpses were apparently left intact, but a sculptured likeness was used as a "reserve head" and buried in a separate chamber of the tomb. In both cases

the apparent intent was to control and protect the souls of the dead
—to exercise power or influence over another person's soul. One
historian suggests that a parallel in contemporary civilization is the
billfold photograph or the framed household photograph of special
friends or family members.[3] Since these likenesses are kept sealed
either on our person or in special frames, it seems likely that some
attempt to control or influence the relationship is intended. Indeed,
these "reserve-head photographs" are often subjected to mutilation
and destruction if they do not perform their intended function satisfactorily (see Fig. 2, 3, and 4).

Perhaps more widespread examples of symbolic control over
unknown forces could be cited in the long history of organized
religion, where art has been used as a vessel through which people
could conceptualize their otherwise nondescript feelings about these
forces; thus exercising a personal—or at least group—control over
them. The history of art is filled with images of gods, and guardians
over death, figures intended to increase fertility, figures intended to
guard crops, and major monuments to serve in man's communication concerning forces existing outside himself. Contemporary man
continues to produce objects intended as visual bridges between the
personal meanings of individuals within groups.

When we approach a work of art, therefore, we might sense
a certain indescribable attraction which may be triggered in one of
many ways (e.g., by a reaction to form, subject matter, material, or
idea). Part of this attraction may come from our collective belief or
faith in man's ability to influence his collective situation. We may
respond to the art work, in part, because of its totemic ability to help
us cope with ideas and situations.

Art As Impulse

In viewing art, we may often be confronted with two works
which seem quite similar in subject matter, picture-plane organization, considerations concerning perspective, color modeling, and
many other ways, yet which evoke quite different feelings or moods.
Subject matter, for example, does not ordinarily provide a complete

Figure 1. *Venus of Willendorf* (c. 25,000 B.C.), stone, 4-3/5″ high. All rights reserved by the Prehistoric Department of the Museum of Natural History, Vienna.

ten

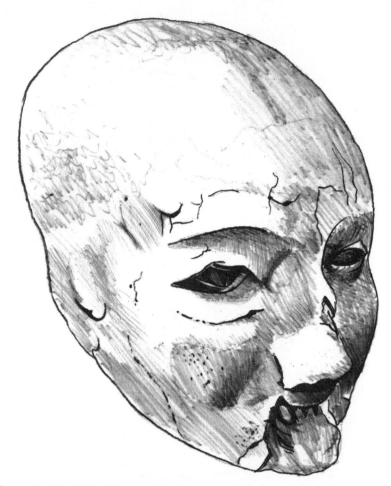

Figure 2. Neolithic Plastered Skull (Jerico head), (c. 7,000–6,000 B.C.), Jerico, Jordan.

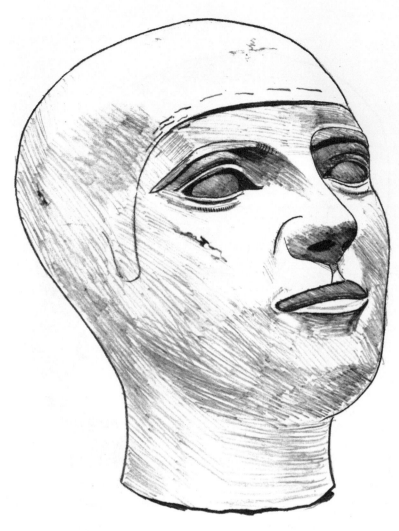

Figure 3.   Reserve Head of a Prince, from Giza (c. 2580 B.C.).

twelve

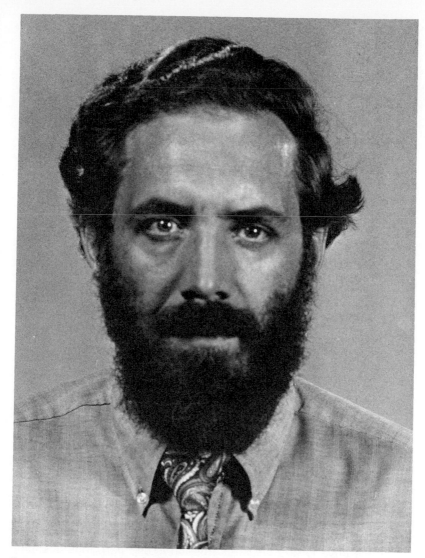

Figure 4.   Contemporary "Reserve Head."

basis for an aesthetic feeling about the work: two entirely different feelings may be evoked from the viewing of two different expressions of the same subject.

Part of the difference may be readily attributable to such things as the color palette or the proportional placement on the canvas of forms and objects. Sometimes the gesture of the figures directly affects the aesthetic outcome. But aside from these obvious indicators there are personal distortions which can only be discerned by very careful observation of the handling of the work. These subtle points of uniqueness evident in art works represent what has been labeled the artist's "style" or his "personal approach" to his work. Although we cannot always attribute certain works to a particular artist on such grounds, it is often possible to make such a connection.

These personal distortions of reality may be due to many factors, the most obvious being the fact that, by virtue of each individual's collection of experiences, no one can view the world in the same way as another. The agreed-upon reality of the visible world is by no means singular; it is peculiar for each human being. Thus any expression of the agreed-upon visible world is bound to be based in private experience and personal distortion. We can expect that each work of art will bring to the viewer a particularity in expression. The individual expression of an experience may be accomplished in many ways. Some communicate experiences through bodily movements, others through verbal interchange, and still others through various combinations of verbal articulation, gestures, facial expressions, and song. Those who study the intricacies of human communications believe that spoken language accounts for a relatively minor portion of human communication. One anthropologist estimates that, on the average, spoken sentences in ordinary conversation last only 2½ to 3 seconds, and that individual verbal communication accounts for only 9 minutes of the day.[4] This means that other forms of communication are extremely important modes of expression in our daily lives. Inarticulate communication, of which the drive toward visual expression is one part, thus accounts for the major portion of human interaction.

Those whose primary impulse is to communicate visually through visual form and visual ideas are called artists. Although most of us sense an impulse to produce visual images, it seems to be a predominant impulse in only a relatively small group—a group which produces images that represent, first of all, the personal or impulsive need to express ideas through visual form, and secondly, the extrapersonal need to communicate through the metalanguage of social archetypes as described under our discussion of magic.

The personal "style" of an artist becomes evident only after viewing a number of his works. This series of "explanations" then become a *style* or way of viewing phenomena, for each artist produces "explanations" of reality which are peculiar to him. There is no way of avoiding the confrontation with the artist's personal vision of reality. It persists beyond the obvious subject material—if he is working honestly toward his own ideas.

Art As Control

It is difficult for us not to expect a certain degree of representation of "reality" in art works, for our impulse to relate the images in the work to previous visual experiences is very strong. One often hears the question from a person viewing an abstract painting, "What is it supposed to be?" And all too often such questions are answered, by those who know better, in an unsympathetic way. Still, the viewer's preoccupation with the "thingness" of an art work often interferes with his recognition of other, more aesthetic considerations. "Objectivity" oftentimes limits appreciation of the work by playing too predominant a role. But having to know what the objects are in an art work is not the only demand placed on art by the novice. It is equally likely that the viewer expects some evidence of skill in production. Not only does man's drive for competence and control represent one of his humanizing qualities, but we are very easily impressed with good craftsmanship.

Questions like "How could he *do* that?" and statements related to "talent" and "beauty" usually follow flourishes of competent production. Many times, however, we are tempted to interpret skill in production as being only applicable to representational realism —that is, to the imitation of natural objects or the use of techniques to "fool the eye" into mistaking manufactured objects for their natural counterparts. But the artist's intention is often quite different. Competency in production may be related to many techniques of which *trompe l'oeil* (illusion) techniques are only a part. Our willingness to expand the definition of competence from imitation of nature to include various picture-plane and application techniques will determine the breadth of our appreciation and the flexibility with which we can assess new and unfamiliar works.

Even competence in achieving representational realism is accomplished in several ways. From utilizing the simple concept of overlapping to using the complex one of geometric and atmospheric perspective is usually a matter of experience alone. Artists who are willing to spend the time required to learn the rules established for effecting atmospheric and geometric perspective can usually learn them; not all artists care to. *Atmospheric perspective* refers to creating the illusion of a three-dimensional surface by reproducing the apparent fadeout of color due to distance. *Geometric or linear perspective* refers to the principle of convergence: when two parallel lines are viewed moving away from us they appear to converge until at last they meet in a point. Should we turn our head slightly, the point of convergence changes. Thus the development of "two-point perspective" to accommodate the physical reality of two eyes, and of "multipoint perspective" to accommodate the possibilities of other ways of seeing.

While these two spatial concepts are useful to representation, other, perhaps more subtle, concepts help account for the technique of "magic realism" or superrealism." One of the most common of these techniques has to do with shading in color or color modeling. Color modeling relies upon a knowledge of the effect of a light source and environment on the shaded portion of an object. Thus an orange fruit in one environment may fade into a brownish shadow with a reflected light of blue coming from objects around it, but in another environment and with a different light the color may fade into violet with a yellow reflected light. The careful study of environments and light can help in achieving sensitive color modeling.

sixteen

When all of these techniques are used and the artist has successfully "tricked" the viewer into mistaking the objects for their real-life counterparts, the problem of individual expression and artistic quality is still not solved. Some "realists" have attained great status in the long history of art, but imitation by itself has never been a guarantee for such recognition. Thus there are other kinds of competence that we must take into account, and even within the realm of perspectivic distortion there are possibilities for the artist to explore a wide variety of views which can either dramatize the subject matter or make it seem quite ordinary. For example, "bird's-eye view" produces a different feeling about the subject matter than a "worm's-eye view" (Fig. 5). Lighting can also be used in dramatic ways—or conversely, in subtle ways. Artists who work within the representational realism mode often explore many means of perspective and color distortions in their search for a personal mode of representation; it is therefore not only possible but fruitful to consider an individual artist's use of these when discussing his "style."

Some artists use these possibilities for effect in highly unique ways, ignoring established rules in favor of their own personal modes of representation. Some try to render the picture plane (the actual two-dimensional surface) so incidental that it virtually disappears, allowing our eyes to move beyond it, into and around the objects in the painting. Usually this involves a careful glazing of the surface which eliminates, as much as possible, the marks of brushes and tools. Other painters work hard to show the unique characteristics of oil paint by building up the surface and taking care that the marks of the brush and other tools are clearly visible. To suggest that the potential is greater for one procedure than for the other is not very satisfactory. Moreover, both procedures require great skill to achieve their effects competently.

Aside from the competencies required in using his tools, processes, and materials and his ability through experience to translate his personal view of objects in a sophisticated—or at least skillful—way, the artist also engages in explorations which have little to do with objects or attempts at representing them. That is, the artist is frequently concerned with relationships within a defined space and the problems associated with the organization of the component

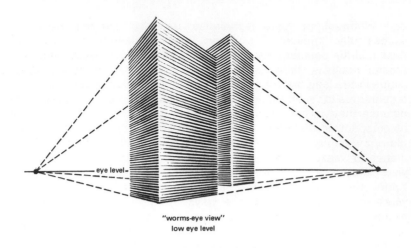

"worms-eye view"
low eye level

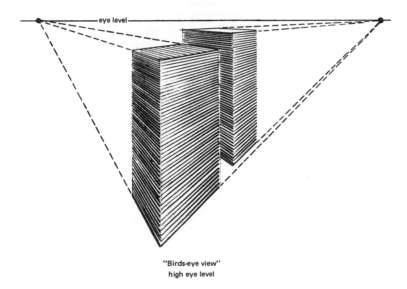

"Birds-eye view"
high eye level

Figure 5.   Two-point perspective.

eighteen

parts of a construction or composition. Attempts at such organization usually begin as a desire to establish a new visual organization by setting aside former design decisions, and are, therefore, not very predictable. Still, attempts at defining the design component of art competence are very strong, and almost any one who has heard of the visual arts has also heard some of the jargon associated with them: texture, value, line, color, and the more abstract concerns of balance, unity, harmony, and the like. The usefulness of these terms is quite limited, however, since they have to be general enough to allow for the establishment of new spatial order. The competence an artist needs to achieve new spatial organizations does not come so much from learning definitions of old spatial order as it does from learning to acknowledge one's personal drive for order based on experience. Some competencies in art are only visible to us when we allow for the uniqueness of organization within a space as compared to a hackneyed or maudlin imitation of other, earlier spatial organizations. Art as control can be viewed in many ways, and our discussion concerning some of these ways is only partially accomplished here. We have identified one (often overused) measure of competence in the use of tools, materials, and techniques for achieving "representational realism." Since this mode is most often subject-bound, it is sometimes difficult to see "beyond" the subject matter and to enjoy the much richer art content. We have suggested that "representational realism" can in and of itself present a variety of possibilities which should not be overlooked. Perspective, color modeling, and the surface technique used by the artist all influence the aesthetic dimensions of the painting of objects, just as such distortions and surface techniques affect our senses in viewing sculpture, graphics, architecture, and the other visual arts. And lastly, we have explored a more illusive definition of competence which is exemplified in a curious drive, not merely for order, but for new order through a gradual disenfranchisement of former orders. Perhaps these short definitions of control can be better explored by discussing and viewing actual works of art. We shall conduct such an exploration in the next part, where each factor in our typology—Magic, Impulse, and Control—will be employed to discuss existing art objects.

SOME HISTORIC AND CONTEMPORARY EXAMPLES

When we consider works of art in terms of the model established in the preceding part, we must once again raise the question of definition, for it will always be possible to redefine—to broaden, shorten, or otherwise change—the original categories to suit our own purposes. Yet it becomes clear that our subsequent definitions may still relate to the use of material and ideas for both expressive and social purposes. We may still wish to discuss objects and other manifestations as curiously unique phenomena, and we may want to communicate concepts and models which to us seem viable in explaining what we feel about them. If the model proposed in the earlier discussion actually promotes or engenders a broader, more expansive view of the phenomenon, then our purposes here will have been served.

twenty

The Two-Dimensional Arts

When we consider the reminders of social necessity which run like a wide ribbon through the history of art, we are struck by the many divergent ways in which groups become necessary. People engaged together in celebration, work, play, ceremony, struggle, or tragedy, have been portrayed in the earliest known recordings of expressive behavior. Even with the move away from subject-oriented material in abstract expressionism, the "groupness" of forms and form interactions have remained a major device.

One example of a painting involving groups of people is the Breughel painting in Fig. 6. We may begin by examining the figures and objects in the painting to see what they are doing and how they are doing it. It is obviously a celebration, and at least more than a family affair. The title, *Peasant Wedding Feast,* leads us into various thoughts which, however, we may reexamine in light of the characterization provided by the artist. If the clothing worn seems foreign, so does, perhaps, the attention to the guests and the nature of the food offerings. What does *not* alienate us is the fact that it is a human enterprise with people engaged together in a ritual feast: the celebration of an event in which two people have established a personal and dual priority in their lives. The people represented in the wedding notwithstanding, the painting has an appeal for other reasons. We may not be particularly interested in "who got married," but rather in the fact that the object (the painting) stands as a totemic reminder of group involvement in things worthy of celebration. It may also provide a vicarious and unconscious control over situations with which we are familiar. Its appeal is at least more than a voyeuristic experience.

The Gericault painting *Raft of the "Medusa"* (Fig. 7) provides a somewhat different totemic reminder of group necessity. The facts surrounding the survivors' ordeal aboard the raft are certainly not conducive to good thoughts about those hapless people bereft of context and survival-oriented. But survival concerns more than the cannibalism it engendered: it also involved rationing and the use

Figure 6. Peter Brueghel, *Peasant Wedding Feast* (1525–1569), Kunsthistorisches Museum, Vienna.

Figure 7. Gericault, *Raft of the Medusa*. Courtesy Cliché des Musées Nationaux.

of sentinels. A single man could not as easily have survived until the rescue ship was sighted (not all did). Aside from the obvious ingenuity required in the raft building, it was the interchange within the group which eventually permitted rescue. The pathos and tragedy of situations involving groups sharing their isolation and despair and building meaning and hope together has been a more-than-random subject in art history. The transactions which occur among people have been, and continue to be, sources of content for artists. We have only to be reminded of the many paintings of people in groups departing, arriving, engaging in ritual and ceremony, witnessing, retreating, and advancing to realize the extent of such glimpses of content. They persist over varied subject matter. But the underlying currents of content which energizes works of art are probably more subtle than the obviousness of groups or aloneness or power or heroism—they probably operate without our conscious awareness of them, even through the most abstruse and abstract forms. The reminder of the condition is there, and it is in this way that the form becomes "magic" in its ability to transcend what we "know" about it. Its energy field is capable of influencing our own by triggering an enjoyment of, or an apprehension about, the nondescript feeling it evokes. Those who cannot consciously relate to such powers outside themselves call these experiences "aesthetic." The marshaling of natural materials into a unification which intensifies the "aesthetic response" to nature results in objects of totemic power—or "art." In this way the social energies which move uncannily among us bind us inextricably to the human family—without them we are not merely alone but, more terribly, alienated. Totems assist in reassurance.

In the Broderson painting (Fig. 8) a different kind of transaction is evident. It is not a totemic reminder of group necessity but instead almost the opposite. We are brought to view a different dimension of our lives—privacy and the dignity of personal reality. We may come to such art ideas as group involvement and aloneness, but only the faintest memory of how they operate within our own existence. There is a sensing, not clearly defined, which triggers some distant echo, causing it to resonate close to our own feelings

Figure 8. Morris Broderson, *Sound of Flowers* (1972), mixed media. Collection: Mr. and Mrs. Neil Rosenstein, Ankrum Gallery.

about things. We cannot, subsequently, identify the true nature of these feelings except in a ost general way. But when we look at certain subject matter—e.g., interpretations of conditional aloneness, groupness, sourceness, or power—we are often moved by our own archetypal responses to them.

The vicarious control over situations and events through art may also be evident in the immediacy of social events. The artist often chooses current events as subject material, and through his skilled and perceptive presentation we are able to "capture" the essence of the event, allowing us to freeze it more securely within our control.

Subject matter, nonetheless, must be only a small portion of this aspect of art, since we respond both culturally and individually to certain images which have no apparent relation to articulated subject matter. Even when we view untitled works of art which are nonrepresentational we may sense some of this same indescribable communication. Forms, by themselves, trigger reminiscences of certain extrapersonal relationships. An example is the artistic use of three objects or three ideas without reference to a particular concept or event. Such arrangements may be obviously connected to such persistent concepts as a triune God, a French love affair, or the Freudian trio (id, ego, and superego); in any case, the deep-seated affinity must surely reside somewhere in the genital origin of such ideas. Man's early concern with the sun, the moon, and the stars is surely manifest somehow in nursery rhymes, ditties, and songs where the deeper idea is buried in such expressions as "rub-a-dub-dub, three men in a tub" and "ready, get set, go," and in such combinations as the three little pigs. These gentle manifestations are persistent, perhaps, because they approach the archetypal conditions common to us all. Whatever they are, they surface in art forms peculiar to a time and culture.

The mythical interpretation of the unknown has a totemic intent, since it presumes to describe, in a tangible way, the parameters of the human condition. But what it might succeed in doing is overthrowing the tyranny of chaos with a fresh ordering—a reassurance that we have, indeed, a means of understanding and power over the gaps in our understanding. To reduce our view of art, however, to any particular group of ideas (including these notions about the use of threes) would seriously limit our ability to view art with feeling. Still, as Jean Luc Godard, once remarked, "reality is too complex; fiction gives it form." Some labels and notions may be required to move to higher positions of appreciation.

In the van Gogh painting *Stairway at Auvers* (Fig. 9) the subject matter is easy to describe, but the anonymity of the walkers moving toward and away from the building is a content which cannot be precisely discussed, since it is intriguing for reasons other than those immediately apparent—just as the Tobey painting *Written Over the Plains* (Fig. 10) may have reminders of our involvement with calligraphy which subtly and incessantly hold our attention.

The second element in our typology, *impulse,* helps us to view an entirely different dimension of the art content of these paintings: personal expressiveness.

The Breughel painting (Fig. 6) maintains some specific distortions of the cubicle space which seem to be an often-used device to accomplish his ideas. A flat, squat cube whose vanishing points skew off the picture plane is shown in Fig. 11. Such a perspectivic device influences all of the objects and figures within the picture plane. Breughel's figures seem imposing and cumbersome, with heavy short bodies and characteristic "workingman's hands." The "weight" of the confinement imposed on the figures produces an almost stooped or hunchbacked posture. The use of such distortion yields a characteristic mode of presentation which is unmistakably Breughel's, although such perspectivic distortion was also used by certain other northern European painters of that time. This distortion combined with a personal use of color and subject matter combine to characterize the impulse which guided the expressive hand of Breughel.

Gericault was schooled in an academic tradition, and the identities we can attribute to him are not as easily discernible. He uses many techniques of the academy, including a strong light source and careful color modeling to achieve a "natural" condition. The uniquenesses we can attribute to Gericault may have more to

Figure 9. Vincent Van Gogh, *Stairway at Auvers* (1890). The St. Louis Art Museum.

twenty-eight

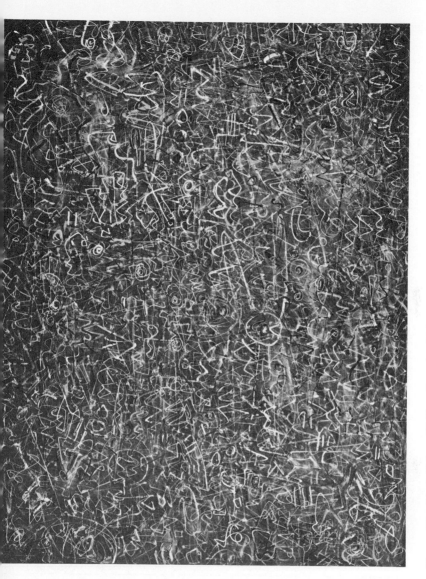

Figure 10. Mark Tobey, *Written Over the Plains* (1950). Gift of Mr. and Mrs. Ferdinand Smith, San Francisco Museum of Art.

Figure 11. Cubicle space distribution in Brueghel's *Peasant Wedding Feast.*

do with his place in history as a turning away from neoclassical subjects and toward emotional contemporary issues. *The Raft of the "Medusa"* (Fig. 7) is important as a major step in the direction of the "spirit of heroic drama," characteristic of the romantic movement to come. Gericault's style is usually associated more with his subject matter choices than with his execution of them, although the exaggerated treatment of his subjects is clearly discernible.

In the Broderson painting (Fig. 8) there is a characteristic softness," an ambiguous space behind the figure which causes us to home in on the specific transaction being undertaken. The title of the painting (*Sound of Flowers*) increases the transcendent nature of the depicted encounter. With Broderson as with certain other mystics, including Morris Graves and Odilon Redon, the fusion between foreground and background produces an immediate electricity, an all-pervasive atmosphere of immediacy and intensity. But Broderson's works differ in tonality, brushwork, placement, and subject matter to the point that it becomes possible to isolate these characteristics as those of one individual. They are Broderson's modes of expressions, which bring to bear the weight of his experiences and particular vision. The longer one studies the work of a single person the more the artist's insights into reality become evident. The viewer, also, participates by applying his own insights —a certain group of options for appreciating art works. The subsequent acceptance of an art work by a large audience may simply mean that the philosophical insights which are projected through the artist's work are approachable over a wider range of viewer perceptions than are other artists' works.

In *Stairway at Auvers* (Fig. 9) we get an immediate sense of van Gogh's particularity in expression. The broad, incessant, contoured brushstrokes coupled with a humanistic portrayal of figures is unmistakeably unique. It is not very difficult to identify the impulsive style of this man. This surety of expression—heavy impasto and deliberate designing of the surface contours—become a direction for a whole new group of artists (the expressionists) at the end of the nineteenth century. But beyond the obviousness of these two stylistic features, van Gogh was a colorist (by his own admission attempting to do in oil painting what the Japanese had succeeded in doing in printmaking). Large brushstrokes of colors, often juxtaposed beside complementary colors, were used to induce a feeling for the entire painting. Van Gogh's is almost a symbolic use of color, though not of the same depth or consistency as Gaughin's or Matisse's. Van Gogh's intent must have been more atmospheric than theirs.

Mark Tobey's work (Fig. 10) like that of Hans Hartung, Jackson Pollack, and Henri Michaux, depends somewhat on its calligraphic nature. But more importantly it seems to stem from a personal commitment toward an open-ended view of the final outcome. For Tobey the act of painting was a process which dictated its direction as it was being formed. It sprang not from visual but from nonvisual perception; it was almost an unconscious dialogue with the process itself, even though Tobey's motivations often came from external sources. Characteristically, Tobey's motifs are often directly related to Chinese calligraphy and religious symbolism and are a mixture of delicate, thin swirling lines and heavy, bold ones.

The accurate identification of the characteristics of individual artists comes from exposure and thoughful viewing. The means by which a viewer identifies these uniquenesses are often different from those projected in a text concerning art and artists. But one of the possibilities for expansive encounters with art objects is to seek out the impulsive base from which the work was formed. Each of these expressions by dint of its uniqueness expands our perception of the world; each provides us with visions other than our own.

The last category within our typology is *control*. Appropriately, the artists discussed thus far are also unique in their approaches to the use of material, tools, and techniques in accomplishing their expressive purposes.

There is a difference in kind when we speak of the control evident in the Gericault painting and control as practiced by either van Gogh or Tobey. Yet to charge that the latter two are incompetent would be in error.

The Gericault painting is not exactly true to his academic training—some small areas of the painting rely on brushed texture for both form and light—but it does remain faithful to the problem of light-dark color modeling.

One kind of control widely practiced in the history of painting and exemplified in *The Raft of the "Medusa,"* is a deliberate attempt to eliminate the picture plane by rendering it invisible. To do this, marks made by painting tools are smoothed and blended into the oil surface. Attempts at realism and naturalism were both quite successful in accomplishing this result. Coupled with the elimination of tool marks is a careful modeling of color, using an extreme directional light source with reflected light coming from nearby objects which backlight the shaded portions. When we view the figures in this painting, we are brought to an awareness of the topological contours of flesh. Gericault's interest in creating the illusion in this particular painting led him to study bodies in a morgue in distended positions, where the bulge and recession of muscle are more evident. The result of such concern with color modeling through the use of directional lighting and reflected light are shown in Fig. 12.

In Gericault's painting, color modeling, a transparent surface, and the use of perspective to create the illusion of distance are evidences of one particular kind of control over materials, tool, and techniques. But a different kind of control is evident in van Gogh's *Stairway at Auvers.* We are not immediately drawn through an invisible picture plane into the painting but instead are encouraged to notice its presence. The picture is being treated in its own right as both a possibility and a limitation of painting. This fact becomes clearer when considered as a move toward more surface considerations in one of the art movements which came about shortly thereafter, *expressionism.* Heavy, built-up paint (impasto) and an attempt to control and direct surface shadows and light were a part of this direction. In addition to the manipulation and use of the canvas surface, van Gogh developed a brush style which took advantage of his knowledge and interest in the color-separation ideas of the impressionists Monet and Pisarro, but which also arose from his own interest in finding equivalents in oil for the block prints of Japanese artistry.

Figure 12. Gericault, *Raft of the Medusa* (detail). Courtesy Cliché des Musées Nationaux.

thirty-four

At first glance, we might be perplexed by any description of Tobey's *Written Over the Plains,* which included the word *control.* There are no "objects" in the painting which we could point to as recognizable, and the seemingly random scribblings do not easily provide us with visual constancies. Aside from the surface considerations which play so great a part in van Gogh's work, there is little obvious reason for referring to this imageless painting as "controlled." But if we move past what might appear to be the obvious and allow ourselves to entertain the ideas with which Tobey was working—and, equally important, to "look carefully" at the painting —we can soon appreciate a different dimension of control: the control of a color palette for expressive purposes; the control of a calligraphic line for symbolic purposes; and the control over the size, length, and curvature of the line forms in consideration of the interplay between them. When abstract expressionism finally removed itself completely from images, these other considerations of control became increasingly important. The differences between competency and incompetency in painting were determined by some new yardsticks.

Another dimension of control which has remained relatively constant throughout the history of art is the control by which the competent development of ideas is accomplished. Every artist works from his own expressive or impulsive base, but not all artists' works express this impulse competently. An artist works steadily and carefully toward the competent control over his own ideas and the means by which to express them.

The Three-Dimensional Arts

Thus far our discussions have been directed more or less to the two-dimensional arts; however, our typology for viewing art is equally useful when applied to the three-dimensional arts of sculpture and architecture. In some ways it is easier to discuss these arts under the category of "magic" as they maintain a life of their own—grasping and holding to themselves a particular cubical space in air. The ability to view them from many different angles—and, in some cases, all the way round—increases the ambiguity of their presence; hence, their power to influence and command the areas into which they are placed. But in addition to this "actual" presence, works of three-dimensional arts have a long history (as old as art history itself) as totemic objects.

The earliest examples of objects and structures appear to have been created for other than trivial purposes. In Fig. 1 we saw the so-called *Venus of Willendorf*—a small, hand-sized pebble which was apparently intended as an amulet to encourage the possibility of human fertility. The perpetual mysteries of death and life provided an impetus toward structures which would reflect man's personal and collective means of control over them. His architecture became his "power" structures whereby a particular hierarchy of godliness could be reinforced through real objects. They became totemic reminders of power which would, with a single glance, affect the allegiance of those who stood before the gate. The Pantheon (Fig. 13), conforming to the social allegiances of its time, was not the "big, beautiful box" that the earlier Parthenon has been called, since its function was quite different from that of the latter structure. The Parthenon was meant to enclose the goddess Athena. The Pantheon was built in honor of *all* the gods and thus required a different conception in construction: room for all of the gods was necessary, and the resulting use of the domed ceiling produced a much larger unencumbered floor space. The structure stood apart from surrounding buildings because of its ability to competently contain that idea.

The cathedral at Amiens (Fig. 14) is representative of a different concept entirely. Huge structures such as these were intended as monumental edifices "in honor of" a single God, not contained therein but residing far away in heaven. Thus the structure was built to reach toward God. It demanded height and floor space enough to contain all the faithful who wished to honor Him.

In medieval Europe the cathedral (and smaller churches) became the virtual center of community activity, occupying the central position in the villages which was for so long held by the castles of

Figure 13. Interior of the Pantheon, Rome. Courtesy Alinari-Art Reference Bureau.

Figure 14. Exterior facade of Notre Dame d'Amiens. Courtesy Archives Photographiques, Paris.

feudal lords. The church became, structurally, a totemic reminder of a powerful social force.

The giant skyscrapers the John Hancock Building (Fig. 15) in Chicago and the twin towers of the World Trade Center (Fig. 16) in New York could also be considered totemic reminders. They are embodiments of the commercial spirit of twentieth-century America and the tremendous power of contemporary technology. Those who stand at their portals must surely sense the same helpless dependence as the twentieth-dynasty Egyptian sensed at the pylons of the temple's of their pharoahs: these huge structures replace, in a real sense, the imperialistic architecture of Washington, which has always stood as an anomaly to the stated intent of the government it houses—a new brand of power.

The TWA Airport Terminal (Fig. 57) designed by Eero Saarinen embodies a spirit of flight—of airiness which can even be sensed as one approaches it on the ground. Sometimes the architect exploits such new possibilities for the sake of the totem, but even so he is probably tied to a social aesthetic, and consequently also expresses the group idea.

Cities, towns, and villages have often grown around the design of the ancient mandala—a magic circle with sections (usually five or seven) radiating from a central core. In Fig. 17 the similarities between this neolithic symbol and the plans for a contemporary city can be seen.

All sculpture is figural in that it occupies a real space, allowing for an ambiguity of presence. Therefore, when sculptural ideas are transfixed in material they are viewed as autonomous objects—or, at least, as actuated ideas—more easily than are two-dimensional presentations. In the Henry Moore sculpture shown in Fig. 18 the caves and mountains of the form not only ring true to the material, but can also trigger faint memories of some of the sources of life itself: mother and earth, or even mother-earth. Moore made no denial of thinking of this connection and often spoke of it. Evidence of this profound interest are his subway sketches produced during the days spent underground in the subways of London during World War II —people wrapped in blankets protected in the womb of the earth

Figure 15. John Hancock Center, Chicago, Illinois. Owner/Developer: John Hancock Mutual Life Insurance Company. Photo by Peter Benton.

forty

Figure 16. World Trade Center. Courtesy The New York Times.

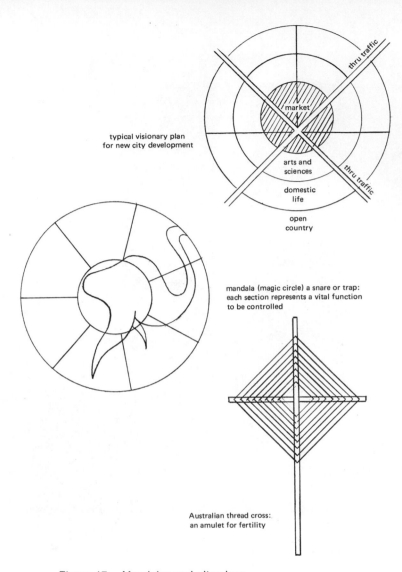

typical visionary plan
for new city development

market

arts and
sciences

domestic
life

open
country

thru traffic

thru traffic

mandala (magic circle) a snare or trap:
each section represents a vital function
to be controlled

Australian thread cross:
an amulet for fertility

Figure 17.   Mandalas and city plans.

Figure 18.   Henry Moore, *Recumbent Figure*. Courtesy The Tate Gallery, London.

away from the reality of German bombs. Moore's totems remind us, perhaps, of these basic and perpetual sources that provide a vicarious assurance of some remote security. Yet the objects may "speak" to different experiences brought to the work by the viewer himself. The sculpture's success is related somewhat to its ability to conjure up possibilities and explanations in the viewer.

The Rodin sculpture *Walking Man* (Fig. 19) presents an armless and decapitated form which is nonetheless very much alive. When Rodin was asked why he made the curious decision to produce the sculpture thus, he replied "A man walks on his feet." Perhaps the strange combination of life and death is the strength of this work, juxtaposing these two conditions in an impossible form. Rodin became convinced of the aesthetic possibilities of such juxtaposition while reflecting on the long history of decapitated heads called portrait busts (for which he also became famous).

This life-death juxtaposition, revived by Rodin, ushered in a long series of such presentations by other artists, among them Maillot, Matisse, Picasso, Appolonius, and Moore. For Rodin, all nature contains semihuman forms, a perception that his form-al extensions from marble and clay often reflect. Many of his human and nonhuman creatures emanate from the elements—a reference not unlike Henry Moore and, much earlier, Michelangelo.

Impulse and its manifestation in architecture has not been as evident in history as it has in the other arts, but with the expansion of technology new materials have provided the contemporary architect with possibilities for such individual expression. It is possible to see the conceptual differences between the structural notions of Frank Lloyd Wright, Mies Van der Rohe, Eero Saarinen, Oscar Niemeyer, and Le Corbusier; but architecture is more often a group enterprise, and involves a greater social input than that found in the other, more privately created arts.

Wright concerned himself with the site upon which the structure was to be built (Fig. 20), an obvious contrast to the designing of a site to meet the aesthetic demands of a structure, exemplified in Niemeyer's Palace Of the Dawn (Fig. 21). Saarinen's unmistakable

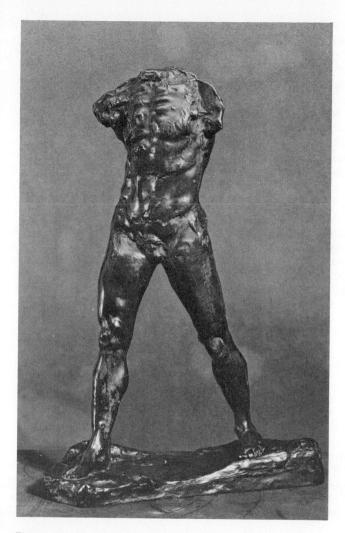

Figure 19. Auguste Rodin, *The Walking Man*, bronze.
Gifts of Mrs. John W. Simpson,
National Gallery of Art, Washington, D.C.

drive toward the use of structural material in an expressive way is also markedly different from Mies van der Rohe's geometric purism —a trademark of the so-called international style. Where Saarinen's modeled concrete produces elegant structural components, Mies van der Rohe is most characterized by his insistence upon austerity ("less is more").

Le Corbusier, although at first a proponent of the "international style," developed quickly and surely toward a more structural use of material. The supports for his creations came to represent more than the austerity of necessity, they became "muscles" for the building, demonstrating the strength of the material itself. In Fig. 22 we can see Le Corbusier's aesthetic more clearly. Structurally, his "house on stilts" requires only posts, but the intent was to express the material as well as to use it.

The sculpture of Henry Moore is at once monumental, massive, and characteristically multiplaned. His interest in the natural surface qualities of stones, the organic growth of material, and the structural alterations produced by natural forces testify to his numinous view of sculptural forms. His works are often left with planes which appear to have been the result of a tremendous shearing force coupled with planes which have been "worn" smooth and rounded over, around, and through the bulk of the material. His impulse toward this "animal vitality" and the erosive characteristics of his material resulted in the unique, massive forms which are easily identified with him.

Rodin became interested in the undulating surface of flesh caused by muscle flexing, bone movement, and strains from contortions, and these preoccupations resulted in his careful surface treatment of "lumps and depressions." His realism is not altogether real but has, rather, a distinctive expressive presence of its own. In *Walking Man* (Fig. 19), the pose is not "real" for walking, since both feet are firmly planted and the muscles of the forward leg appears to be as engaged as the rear one. Rodin was interested in the forms themselves as much as in their "storytelling" functions. His interest

Figure 20. Fallingwater. Photo by Michael Fedison. Courtesy Western Pennsylvania Conservancy.

Figure 21. Temple of Dawn, Brazilia. Courtesy Von Keuol/Katherine Young.

Figure 22.   Corbusierhaus, Berlin. Courtesy Katherine Young.

was to eliminate all that which would draw attention away from the essential or "leading" idea.

> "As to polishing nails or ringlets of hair, that has no interest for me, ... it detracts attention from the leading lines and the soul which I wish to interpret.... One must have a consummate sense of technique to hide what one knows."[5]

And this combination of "leading line" and "consummate technique" resulted in a characteristic Rodin expression.

Technique develops from experience and eventually leads to the ability to *control* tools, materials, techniques, and ideas so that the impulsive distortions of the artist are freed from uncertainty.

In architecture control is often tied to characteristics of materials and technological development. Architecture is a very precise art demanding careful attention to the strains produced by compression (weight of material on material) and tension (outward thrust created by spans between posts). Therefore, the architect must understand the relationships of mass to weight, the properties of materials, the nature of the building site—including the terrain and soil characteristics—and, often the costs of construction. Only beyond the mechanics of such information is the architect free to exploit both materials and idea.

The development of the "round arch" gradually replaced the use of "corbeled arches" (see page 142) and provided for new interior possibilities, just as the eventual development of the dome increased the space available for designing the interior of buildings.

Materials development was, in part, instrumental in permitting the designing and modeling of forms by Le Corbusier and Saarinen. The control over a particular use of a material or an idea is somewhat different from the general mastery required for building alone, and we must take into account these individual competencies as they exist in architecture.

Saarinen's control (for example) over line and form can only become real when we physically move in, through, and around the actual structures, since he was cognizant of the "vistas" or views which emerge from every point and juxtaposed these elements to provide for anticipatory glimpses. A view of his work from a photograph cannot do justice to the dimension of control over these curvilinear "vistas." On the other hand, the control exhibited by Le Corbusier can be more readily appreciated from a photograph, since each structural unit exhibits the musculature that he intended.

In architecture and city planning, as well as in the other arts, control and its subsequent manifestations should not be overlooked as we approach and experience them.

The personal approach to material in sculpture produces specific instances of competence and control, so that it is possible to enjoy the same material and process through differing kinds of treatment.

In the Henry Moore figure the rounding of forms, as if eroded by natural causes, contrasts sharply with the polished surfaces of a Brancusi or an Arp—although the "control" Moore exercises over his stones is no less sophisticated. His ability to produce surfaces and planes which appear to have been sheared and ground by nature herself requires an energy equal to that expended in polishing the stone. The difference, therefore, is not in Moores' inability to achieve a polished-type surface, but rather in his relentless drive away from that kind of surface.

The Rodin sculpture begins not with exterior forces acting upon the surface but with interior forces—moving and undulating, and consequently influencing the surface characteristics. The competent development of this idea required no less energy or commitment, but it was obviously in response to a different aesthetic calling. And although Henry Moore maintained a more-or-less numinous view of his material, Rodin expressed this same numen quality by a more romantic and freshly formed appearance to his figures by effecting a peculiar combination of human form and nebulous mass, the former being extruded from the latter. The problems inherent in the control of material and idea were, therefore, substantially different for these sculptors.

Our typology—*Magic, Impulse,* and *Control*—has been useful perhaps, in the development of a means by which to begin to approach and experience art, but it will undoubtedly leave many dimensions of the complex functions and purposes of art untapped as our experience with art increases. And it is not adequate, perhaps, to discuss certain other obvious characteristics and distinctive properties of art as manifest in the materials themselves. In the next part we shall outline some of the distinctive properties of the methods and materials through which artists formulate their work.

MATERIALS, TOOLS, AND PROCESSES

Each material chosen by an artist to formulate his ideas has its own distinctive and resistant properties. A granite or marble stone requires an approach quite different from oil and canvas, and the finished work is not only unique in its use of actual space but is also distinctive in the methods by which it was produced and the total effect of those procedures. Our understanding of these distinctions within and among the arts may provide us with one more dimension of appreciation when we view the art object, since the total effect of the art work is affected by the individual qualities of the medium and the characteristics of the technique.

The artist deliberately chooses the material to suit his expressive needs. In some cases he may, out of curiosity, redo the same artistic idea in another medium or process. The artist's decision whether to carve, paint, draw, or etch has an important influence on the expressive outcome of the work. And within each of the materials and techniques there are many variations which produce differing expressive results.

We shall attempt to review here each of six arbitrary divisions within the arts—drawing, sculpture, painting, graphics, architecture, and the "minor arts"—discussing the characteristics which make them unique or different from each other; for even though we have already discussed the similarities between these divisons, we hope to establish many distinctive features which can also be observed. Secondly, we shall explore the materials and processes themselves —the tools and how they are used.

Drawing

Since early man made his first impulsive gestures in clay and developed his linear symbols for communicative purposes, drawing has been an important means of visually expressing ideas. Not only is it a precursor of language (young people produce greater amounts of visual material—before language equivalents replace some of this function—than do adults), but it also maintains a language of its own. Drawing means the making of lines, and we have all from our earliest years been involved in line making of one sort or another. This fact makes drawing perhaps the most intimate of all of the arts. To be confronted by a drawing seems in many ways to bring us a little closer to the initial act of creation. Perhaps this is because line is an invention of man himself. Lines in nature exist only when we see two planes converge or when we impose a linear quality on the edge of an object. Thus the actual development of line has been related to man and his art and, unlike the other visual elements, line exists only as we ourselves form it.

In art, drawings may generally be thought of in one of two ways. First, they may be preliminary visualizations intended as working models for work to be done in other materials or media. These may be described as *sketches, studies,* or (as in the case of very large preliminary drawings which eventually are covered up with the finishing material) *cartoons*. Secondly, drawings may be finished works in and of themselves.

Drawing as a preliminary investigation into form, gesture, and value on a reduced or miniature scale is called *sketching*. We may get some feeling for the sketch if we consider our own involvements in the activity called "doodling." Usually such attempts are hardly serious enough to classify as sketches, yet they are efforts intended to establish a certain relationship between figure and ground. The intent in doodling seems to be to establish figures within a specified ground area. The artist who sketches is concerned with this same relationship when his visual transformation of an experience is done "on the spot" or "on an impulse." One may view the Rembrandt Van Rijn drawing (Fig. 23) as an example of a sketch. In this particular drawing, Rembrandt has established the figure-ground *(form)* relationship that he felt was satisfactory and he further established the *gesture* or stance of the figures by directional lines. He also established the *value* relationships which he felt were essential.

If we look at the Rembrandt sketch and try to ignore the subject matter so that the relationship between the foreground forms and the background forms (figure and ground) becomes evident, we can see that the artist has provided us with an interesting and dynamic relationship within the picture plane. A strong relationship exists between the forms or *figures* and the areas around the forms or the *ground*. Of course, many other factors affect our feeling about this relationship, and we must be careful not to isolate this aspect of our analysis from all other aspects. But one of the early concerns of the artist when he makes his preliminary marks on a surface is to establish this *figure-ground* relationship. This occurs in all of the arts, although it is most pronounced in the two-dimensional forms— drawing, painting, and graphics. One may refer to this preliminary search for form within space as one aspect of the sketch.

A second concern of the artist in his sketch may be to establish the positioning of the figures or objects. This is referred to as *gesture*. Gestures which provide for anticipation or incomplete action often accompany the preliminary drawings or sketches of

Figure 23. Rembrandt, *Nathan Admonishing David*. Bequest of Mrs. H.O. Havemeyer, 1929; the H.O. Havemeyer Collection, The Metropolitan Museum of Art.

fifty-six

the artist and are considered to be extremely important in the establishment of a satisfactory form. It is easy to see that many more such possibilities existed for the artist. The skillful, determined hand of Rembrandt, however, produced this particular gesture for the figures in his drawing. His judgment, in this instance, for expressing the idea he had in mind is one of the many reasons for ranking him highly in the history of art. In his considered judgment he had achieved the gestural positioning he desired.

A third and perhaps somewhat less important aspect of the preliminary sketch is the decision made relative to the placement of darks and lights in the composition. The artist sometimes establishes dimensionality by pressing on the drawing tool and forcing back the line when he wishes to achieve depth or distance. In our discussion of aerial or atmospheric perspective we found the exact opposite to be the case. That is, the "lightness" or the "greying" of objects or forms gave the appearance of distance. But in drawing we find that the darker, wider line often provides the depth required to articulate the third dimension. Aside from depth, however, *value* establishes relationships within the picture plane itself. The establishment of these values seems to be an important part of some artists' preliminary visualization of experience. Its effect upon the relationship of the parts to the whole is certainly important.

The *study* is somewhat different in intent from the sketch, although it may also be "preliminary" to a more sophisticated technique. Studies may be small or they may be quite large. The intentional difference in the study is that it involves careful and deliberate articulation of the particulars of a sketch. Instead of establishing *general* form, gesture, and value, the study establishes *specific* form, gesture, and value. Usually these gradations include the refinement of form which is based upon a careful analysis of the original figure-ground relationship and the secondary or specific forms within the original figure-form. In many instances one can see in completed drawings a few of the lines still showing from the original sketch, suggesting that the artist has selected, from among the many sketch lines, which ones will be sustained in the *study* (see Fig. 24).

Figure 24. Edgar Degas, *Portrait of Emile Duranty*. Rogers Fund, 1918, The Metropolitan Museum of Art.

fifty-eight

The study is strongly guided by the sketch, since by definition it is a refinement. Therefore, we can assume that the gesture and form established by the sketch will essentially hold true for the study. The value structure, however, may be altered extensively. The intent of the study is to clarify, in as analytical a way as possible, the configuration of the defined figure; and since modeling a form from dark to light and providing dark values to increase textural contrasts does provide the artist with a means of presenting his artful observations, value becomes a very important component of the study. A study may be only a portion of the sketch or only a portion of the intended work, yet it provides the artist with a means of solving certain questions he may have before he begins the final work. Studies may be smaller versions of the work to come or they may represent the actual size intended for the painting (see Fig. 25).

Sometimes sketches and/or studies are actually drawn on the surface prepared for painting and the finished work is painted directly on top of the drawing. In this case, the underdrawing is referred to as a *cartoon*. Cartoons are also drawn on one surface and then transferred to another surface. They are more like large sketches than large studies, although the artist may delineate some portions of the sketch before beginning to paint.

Drawings may also be finished works in and of themselves, such as is evident in much of the drawing of Oriental origin. Many of the hanging scrolls and ink drawing on colored silks were intended to be complete works (see Fig. 26). Viewing drawing as completed works of art has historically been a non-European trait dating to about 1000 B.C. The earliest examples of European work which is clearly in this tradition seem to be related to the development of the etching and engraving processes early in the fifteenth century A.D.

The continued interest in and appreciation of the qualities of drawing has resulted in many calligraphic works in the twentieth century which are drawings intended as completed works (see Fig. 10).

Drawings can be done in many different materials, and we shall discuss some of the more common ones here, but before we begin we should examine some of the surfaces upon which drawing

Figure 25.   Leonardo da Vinci, Sketches for the Madonna. Rogers Fund, 1917,
The Metropolitan Museum of Art.

sixty

Figure. 26.   Sesshu, *Haboku Landscape*.
The Norweb Collection, The Cleveland
Museum of Art.

is done. The expressive outcome of a work is affected by the nature of the surface upon which the drawing is placed. A very smooth surface will produce a different pencil line than a surface which is textured. In some instances the surface is restricted to a particular quality by the drawing medium. Silverpoint, for instance, demands a surface hard enough to receive the pressure required to leave a silver line and textured enough to encourage the deposit. Other media, such as ink because of its fluid quality, can be applied to many surfaces. It should be noted here, however, that there have been many instances in the history of art where the availability of desired surfaces was limited, and many charming drawings have been executed on such esoteric materials as squared notepaper, cardboard, cloth, and wood. Given an assortment of choices, however, the artist considers the expressive possibilities of the surface upon which he draws and in some instances spends a good deal of time preparing a surface before the drawing tool touches it.

The Carbons. Carbon is one of the most versatile elements on earth. It combines readily with other elements and it is relatively easy to separate out from many compounds. Carbon, in one form or another, is a part of all organic material. It can be found in its natural state in two forms: diamond and graphite. By burning organic material under controlled conditions it can also be produced in relatively pure states such as lampblack (soot), boneblack, charcoal, and coke.

Whether or not the charred remains of a fire served as an impetus toward the development of our first writing instruments is obviously speculative, yet it is tempting to make such a connection. We can be quite sure, at least, that *charcoal* represents one of the most ancient of the drawing materials still in use today. It is now produced in convenient form by confining small, close-grained twigs or roots in sealed containers which are baked to a temperature high enough to char the contents but low enough to prevent open-flame combustion. The result is a more-or-less pure carbon stick. This process was originally done with the roots of the grapevine, which produces a fine-quality drawing charcoal. To this day, charcoal produced from these roots is referred to as "vine charcoal." Most commercial operations today do not make vine charcoal, however, since a relatively good-quality stick can be produced from other sources such as twigs from the willow tree.

By grinding large pieces of charcoal and then compressing the charcoal powder, another form of drawing instrument is produced. This "pressed charcoal," however, produces a much darker line which seems to have more of the quality of the black crayon as used by artists of the Italian Renaissance (as opposed to the familiar wax-impregnated crayon) than it does the qualities of charcoal.

Charcoal may range from a very soft stick (a larger-grained and higher-baked stick which produces deeper blacks) to a very-fine-grained lower-fired stick which produces lighter-valued lines (see Fig. 27).

The early uses of charcoal were apparently limited to sketches and cartoons, since no means of preserving them was probably available before the eighteenth century. Many "fixatives" are available today to prevent smearing or smudging. The charcoal, although it is readily received by most surfaces, has a propensity toward smearing. In the hands of the artist it can be one of its qualities, but for preserving works done in charcoal, some protection is needed against undesirable marks and fingerprints.

A second drawing tool made from the carbons is the *pencil.* We often assume that the common writing pencil is composed of lead filler with a wooden, plastic, or pressed paper sheathing, but in actuality the material is not a metal at all. It is the substance called *graphite,* a pure form of amorphous carbon with a metallic luster. In its natural state it is either too hard or too flaky to make it very practical as a drawing material; thus it remained for technology to develop a means by which it could be utilized effectively.

The pencil as we know it today is less than two hundred years old. It was developed by the Frenchman N. J. Conte around 1795. In the Conte process fine particles of clay and graphite are combined using water as a catalytic binder. The mixture is then baked or "fired" until the clay forms a bond for the graphite particles. The result is well known to us. Most of our writing pencils are produced

Figure 27.   Pablo Picasso, *Nude*. The Alfred Stieglitz Collection, 1949, The Metropolitan Museum of Art.

in this fashion. Graphite-clay mixtures are produced in both pencil form (from a very-hardbaked density for light-valued lines to very-softbaked low-clay mixture, which produces the darker values) and stick form (referred to as *graphite sticks*), both of which are used for broad strokes and finely graduated values from black to pale grey (see Fig. 28).

Graphite, even in its purest form, does not produce the deep blacks of carbon in other forms such as the charcoals and lamp-blacks because of its peculiar metallic luster. A single, unobtrusive mark of charcoal on a pencil drawing is easily and quickly spotted since the dull surface of a charcoal line immediately contrasts with the luster of the graphite.

Minerals. With the advent of printing presses in the fifteenth century came a demand for paper. Paper mills were widely established by the early sixteenth century, and drawing, as it is known today, began.

The search for usable natural materials which could provide for colored drawings and intense blacks resulted in the discovery of two important native Italian stones which could be processed into writing-size instruments and applied to paper.

The first was a native black slate which has come to be known as Italian black crayon or black chalk.

The second important mineral to be mined and used as drawing material is hematite or bloodstone, which has come to be called Italian red crayon or red chalk. Its French name, *sanguine,* is often used in reference to drawings done in hematite (Fig. 29). The cartoon was often an underdrawing of *sanguine.* Many full-scale drawings were also executed at this time.

Chalk is often processed directly from a soft limestone made up of decomposed shells of foraminifers. It has a natural coloring from white or grey to buff. Hard chalks are produced under pressure much like pressed charcoal.

Attempts at achieving a proliferation of colors in chalk were essentially unsuccessful, but the effort led to the use of the Conte process of combining fine clay particles with many different pigments, resulting in a wide range of clay crayons. It was not until the

Figure 28. Pablo Piscasso, *Ambroise Vollard* (1867–1939).
Elisha Whittelsey Collection, 1947, The Metropolitan Museum of Art.

Figure 29. Michelangelo, *Study for the Libyan Sibyl*.
Joseph Pulitzer Bequest, 1924, The Metropolitan Museum of Art.

eighteenth century, however, that such combinations came into wide use.

The most sophisticated development in chalk arose from experiments combining chalk, pigment, and gum binders, which provided for most colors in many tints and tones. The product of this research became known as the *pastel*. Many works in the eighteenth century were done in pastels. The Degas drawing in Fig. 30 is one fine example of the pastel.

Many times we find that pastels are exhibited under glass. This is so because unlike the crayon or the carbons, pastels react and change when a fixative is applied unless the fixative is very fine and applied lightly. Thus most artists prefer to protect pastels with glass.

Besides chalks, there is another group of mineral-based drawing tools called the *wax crayons.* The term *crayon* is technically applicable to any prepared writing or drawing tool and was used interchangeably with the term *chalk* for hundreds of years. The Conte crayon, for instance—which is still sold under that name— is a clay-and-gum-based chalk very similar in mixture to the hard pastel. Still, when we speak of the *crayon* we most often mean the wax crayon. The wax crayon is probably the least used of the drawing tools available today, although there are fine instances of its usability. Instead of the clay or gum binders used in chalks and pastels, the wax crayon utilizes various mixtures of beeswax, paraffin, and petroleum products. A wide range of color is possible with a much greater choice of intensities. Brilliant and lasting colors are possible when pigments are imbedded in wax.

The Metals. Since graphite was not available for general use before around 1800, metallic surface drawings before that time were as a rule made with thin rods of metal which were sharpened and held in a stylus. Silver was most popular for drawing, whereas lead was popular for writing. The surface upon which *silverpoint* drawing is accomplished is usually prepared with a fine powdered abrasive such as tin oxide or bone size in order to receive a deposit of silver. Unlike lead or graphite, silver deposited on such a surface is extremely difficult to erase. Thus the artist moves carefully and de-

Figure 30.   Edgar Degas, *The Tub*. Cabinet des Dessins Musée du Louvre. Cliché Musées Nationaux.

liberately across the surface. Silverpoint is not only characterized by calculation and the use of even, fine lines, but often by its use of reticular surfaces to build up values (see Fig. 31).

When first applied, the silver produces a light grey line. After exposure to light or after a period of time it reacts to the sulphides in the atmosphere and begins to turn tan or brown. This oxidation process is often speeded up by intensifying the acid fumes artificially.

The use of silverpoint has a long history dating to the Middle Ages, and although not widely used today will probably continue to provide its characteristic expressive quality to those artists who demand it.

The Inks. There is a group of drawing materials which are formulated in a liquid state or in a solid state intended for liquid application. Some of them are carbon-based and some of them are mineral-based. Inks have been known and used for some 2,000 years. Ancient carbon-based Chinese ink sticks and liquid india ink remain to this day the most popular of black inks. They are made from specially selected grades of lampblack combined with a binding solution (in some instances, perfume).

Mineral-based inks produce a wide range of colored inks, although they have largely been replaced with modern chemical dyes.

During the Renaissance, an ink produced from the burning of certain trees containing tar resins, called *bister*, was quite popular. Its color is varied not only by its application but also by the peculiarities of the resin. The range is generally from yellow to a dark reddish brown. Bister is used both with pen and brush since, like the carbon inks, it can produce values over a wide range from very light to dark.

The ink sacs of the squid from the Mediterranean Sea provide a source for another popular ink, *sepia*, which is a semitransparent, rich brown ink especially in vogue around the end of the eighteenth century. The popularity of sepia and bister ended with the rising availability of less esoteric products, until today it is extremely difficult if not impossible to locate suppliers of either.

Figure 31.   Pavel Tchelitchew, *Portrait of Frederick Ashton*. Gift of Meta and Paul J. Sachs, courtesy of the Fogg Art Museum, Harvard University.

The quality of inks is highly dependent upon the surface to which they are applied and the techniques used in the application. Wet or dry surfaces, full-strength or diluted ink, brushes or pens are all important considerations to the artist, since they will affect the expressive outcome to a greater degree in ink drawing than in any other drawing media (see Fig. 32).

Sculpture

It is somewhat more difficult to discuss the unique characteristics of sculpture, since they are integrally related to our experience with a work as real object. Sculpture is three-dimensional and exists in a real cubical space. This fact should help us to appreciate sculptured works more easily because we experience most objects in this way. Still, we are handicapped somewhat when we try to discuss the third dimension because in print we are confined to two-dimensional representations of cubical space.

The most we can do is to rely on our ability to intellectualize about space and to try to imagine our examples here as they would appear in real space.

There is an aspect of space development in sculpture which mere three-dimensionality does not take into account. Sculpture defines a particular and more aesthetic space than a random object. It may command a courtyard or it may require a less confining space such as a field. It may demand a niche in a garden or cathedral or it may be aesthetically suited to a fountain area. When we consider the Henry Moore sculpture in Fig. 18 we are impressed with how it confines its presence to the stone whence it came. The space it defines outside itself is much less expansive than the Rodin figure in Fig. 19. In Rodin's sculpture, the space becomes ambiguous in front of the figure and more or less tenuous around the rest of the figure.

A second characteristic of sculpture has to do with its tactile nature. Although visual texture is produced in most art, sculpture in particular invites the touch of both smoothness and roughness.

Figure 32. Henry Moore, *Madonna and Child* (1943). Hinman B. Hurlbut Collection, The Cleveland Museum of Art.

Public statuary are often polished in certain reachable and desirable areas because people feel a need to touch them. In museums, however, very few textures—smooth or rough—on paintings, drawings, graphics, or crafts are touched by the public. These works could not take the physical wear that sculpture does; moreover, museum officials generally look askance on such a practice, for fear of breakage or damage. But even without these considerations it seems that sculpture appeals to the sense of touch more than two-dimensional work. Rodin increased this appeal by leaving the gouges of tools and the raw marks of fingers and molds in much of his work.

Sculpture also has many unique aspects within itself as far as material and processes are concerned. The way an artist approaches a material determines, to a great extent, the expressive outcome. Approaches to producing the sculpture tend to relate to four different procedures: subtraction, construction (or addition), modeling, and substitution. The procedures the artist decides upon directly affect his expressive approach and the expressive outcome of the work.

The *subtractive process* is essentially carving, usually done in stone or wood. Although a great deal of carving has been done in ivory and shell, most carved works of major status have been in the former materials. With this process the artist must "see" into the material as he works, for any material that he removes often cannot be satisfactorily replaced, although many examples of work done by the subtractive process are also constructions (see Fig. 33). In these cases, the basic wood blocks have been made larger by pegging wood additions onto it. Today, stoneworkers also attach stones together with chemical epoxy bonding. It is important to remember that artists themselves are not committed to use one or the other of our categories, but may combine different processes and materials at will. Our use of categories here is primarily to help to establish how a particular work was done to help explore the general characteristics of both the process and the material.

Carving is essentially a process of removing edges. Sometimes the edges are defined prior to carving—drawn on all sides of the

Figure 33.　King Se'n Wosret I wearing the crown of Lower Egypt. From the tomb of Imhotep, Lisht. The Metropolitan Museum of Art, Museum Excavations, 1913–1914; Rogers Fund supplemented by Contribution of Edward S. Harkness.

material to establish the relationship of the form to be released with the material to be cut away. This is not always done, however. Viewing the Michelangelo carving in Fig. 34 we get an unusually clear indication that Michelangelo sensed the form within the stone without preliminary drawing on the block. His "form release" was direct, moving into the stone to the final surface without articulating his form from the other sides. In either case, however, the artist relies upon some predetermination of form when he chooses carving. The form may change during the process, but a general direction is important to him.

There is a "grain" in both wood and stone which determines to some extent the directional form for the artist. The structure of wood is circular and produces curvilinear lines when carved, whereas stone inclusions in the bedline are layered and maintain their layered appearance after carving. The diagrams in Fig. 35 demonstrate this difference. Artists who work with grained wood or stone must consider the expressive qualities of the material when choosing carving as a process.

The *additive process* is related in some ways to drawing and painting, since it is a build-up process. In this process the artist is free to move into an air space, limited only by his concept or plan for the form. The finished work, whether plaster of paris, wood construction, or welded construction, contains expressive elements peculiar to the process.

Problems of construction influence to a great extent the generative nature of the finished work. To construct, the artist begins on the inside moving outward; thus we can observe the projective freedom which is evident in much of constructed work (see Fig. 36).

Modeling is done with material which is plastic enough to allow movement in all directions. Common materials used in the modeling process are clay, wax, plaster, and plastic impregnated with fillers. This process is the most tactile of all, since the sculptor works very close to the surface, in some cases molding the material in his hands. The results of such intimate contact become evident as we view the Rodin work in Fig. 37. Here the obviously intricate surface characteristics of "lumps and depressions" pro-

Figure 34. Michelangelo, *Boboli Slave*.
Courtesy Alinari-Art Reference Bureau.

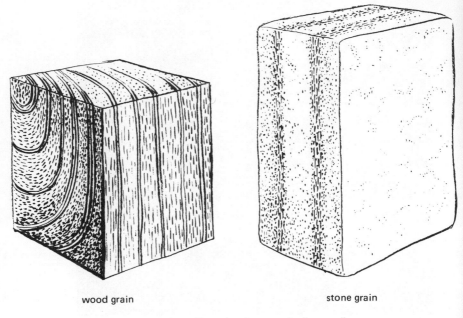

wood grain   stone grain

Figure 35.   Wood grain (curvilinear); stone grain (layered).

Figure 36. Welded construction piece "Fountain." Stainless steel. Yar Chomicky. Photograph by Merle Cutler.

Figure 37.   Auguste Rodin, *The Walking Man*, detail. Gift of Mrs. John W. Simpson, National Gallery of Art, Washington, D.C.

eighty

duce a different visual surface than do the carved or constructed surfaces in our previous examples. In addition, each modeling medium produces its own characteristic surface. It might be well for us to compare the Degas wax figure (Fig. 38) with the Rodin. Modeled wax is different from modeled clay, each having its own unique elastic properties. The artist chooses a material for modeling with these properties in mind.

Substitution processes are often directly related to both modeling and construction processes. The artist may decide that he wishes his original sculpture to be cast in a more permanent material or he may wish to produce an edition (group of copies) of it. In these instances, the original material is replaced, through various mold-making procedures, with the desired finish material. The reproduction is only faithful to the extent that shrinkage is avoided in the finished casting. With those materials which produce only exothermic heat (such as plaster or plastic) the shrinkage in the cast is negligible; however, metal shrinkage and the very large loss of volume in clay pieces materially affect the overall dimensions of the work—consequently its expressive outcome. The artist who chooses a substitution procedure must consider the possibility of volume change in these materials.

In the next few pages we shall discuss certain of the materials and processes used by the sculptor. Although technological advances and the move away from traditional materials have shifted the current sculpture scene to predominantly construction techniques, it may serve our purposes best to use four major production procedures to discuss sculpture: carving, joining, modeling, and casting.

Carving Tools and Techniques. The wood carver selects, from among the various trees available, those woods which will carve evenly, are close-grained, and will allow the production of textures ranging from gouge depth to a smooth polish. In general, the hardwoods are used, since splintering is minimal and the carver is free to work in more than one direction. In addition, the hardwoods can be brought to a high polish when desired. Some typical woods which meet these requirements are ebony, walnut, coco-bolo, elm, and cherry.

Figure 38.   Edgar Degas, *Statuette: Developpe en avant*, bronze. Bequest of Mrs. H.O. Havemeyer, 1929, The Metropolitan Museum of Art.

The preparation of the wood is very important to the carver, since improperly prepared wood can crack open or "check" and/or resist finishes. Usually the wood is dried by removing the bark and waxing the ends. In this way the drying time and drying distribution are controlled. Controlled drying produces fewer and smaller "checks." Once the carver has begun, he may also continue to wax the carved surfaces after each carving session. Wood that is not dry will also resist even finishes. It is therefore quite important not only to dry the wood but to dry it properly before carving. The initial carving tools used in this process consist of a gouge and a wooden mallet. In Fig. 39 the gouges and mallets used for wood carving are identified. The size of the carving and the preferences of the artist determine to some extent the size and the shape of the gouges and mallets used.

Beyond the use of gouges, finishing tools for wood include the rasp and abrasive paper, from coarse grit to fine. Waxes, stearine, and turpentine or lacquer are often used to seal and develop a sheen or polish on the finished work.

The stone carver selects from among a variety of stones which have been used successfully for carving. These include granite, a very hard rock of metamorphic origin produced under intense heat and pressure; marble, a much softer stone which is highly carvable and universally available; sandstone, a stone much less used today than previously; steatite, jade, alabaster, and some forms of quartz which are easily carvable but not available in large quantity. Marble has been, by far, the most popular of these stones, perhaps because it is highly carvable, comes in a variety of hardnesses, and is widely available. Large deposits of marble occur in most major countries. Certain deposits have become famous for the marble produced by them. The seemingly unlimited supply of Greek marbles produced from about 600 b.c. to about 100 b.c. were drawn from two major quarries, the Pentellic and the Pariah. Italian sources have been in Carrara and Siena since around 100 B.C. to the present. In North America, the eastern seaboard from Maine to Alabama represents a huge and variegated source of marble.

Many very large statues have been produced from marble.

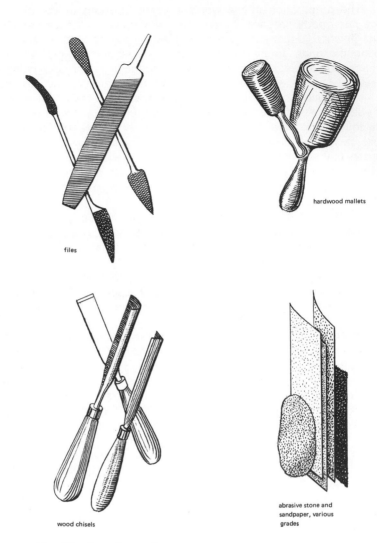

files

hardwood mallets

wood chisels

abrasive stone and
sandpaper, various
grades

Figure 39.   Wood-carving tools.

eighty-four

One example is the compelling statue of David, produced by Michelangelo when he was twenty-six years of age. This immense work stands 13 feet 5 inches high and was carved from a block of stone which must have weighed approximately thirty-two thousand pounds. Some have speculated that this work was "pointed up" or enlarged mechanically, although there is no evidence to support such a claim. This procedure for enlarging, however, has been used extensively in the history of sculpture. It is based upon the idea of a machine which translates proportion. The smaller model is carefully scanned with a needle arm attached to an elongated arm which measures depth and relationships within the huge block of stone. Drills are used to identify the contour of the finished piece. These drill holes are produced over the entire huge block before carving takes place. The excess material is then removed and the finishing done either by the artist himself or his appointed assistants.

The tools for carving marble are somewhat different from wood tools. The hammer used is made of iron, and the tools for chipping are a series of "points" (pointed chisels) and "rakes" (toothed chisels). The "bull chisel" is used for removing large chunks of unwanted material, whereas the graduated points are used for roughing out the form. The toothed chisels are then employed to further refine the form and to get below the bruise marks produced by the points. In Fig. 40 the various tools used by the stone carver are shown.

Finishing a stone is quite similar to finishing wood. Rasps are used to bring the toothed–chisel marks down to the final surface. Silicon carbide grit papers are then used to gradually bring the surface to a polish. The final polish is usually accomplished with tin oxide or pumice powder together with water on a chamois or goatskin.

Joining Procedures and Tools. Perhaps the oldest joining device in the history of construction is the peg: one piece is formed with a protruding part which fits snugly into a recessed hole in the second piece. Our Egyptian example in Fig. 33 represents an early use of this device. Metal pegging was often done where large bronzes were required. These statues were cast in several sections and then joined by notching and pegging.

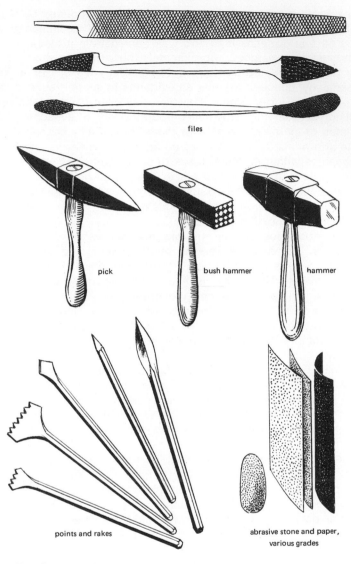

files

pick   bush hammer   hammer

points and rakes   abrasive stone and paper, various grades

Figure 40.   Stone-carving tools.

The use of glues, cements, and other bonding agents is often combined with pegging, but just as often they are used as primary fastening materials. Early forms of glue were simple animal gelatins obtained by boiling the skins, bones, and hoofs of animals. When heated with water they provide a liquid glue for attaching many kinds of materials. Other glues are obtained from milk products and eggs. Large sections of wood forms are often accomplished by the use of glues. In the sculpture shown in Fig. 41 a milk-product glue was used to provide the artist with a spatial freedom not possible with carving alone.

Chemical binding agents have now been developed which provide the artist with many more possibilities for construction. In the marble construction-carving in Fig. 42 a specially formulated epoxy-resin agent was used to cantilever heavy stones out and away from the base pieces. Such exploitation of technology has greatly expanded the use of traditional materials and caused the process divisions to be defined in a more general way. Other joining processes which have been used extensively (especially in the twentieth century) are soldering and fusion or welding.

Soldering is the term used to describe the flowing of a second metal between the two pieces of metal to be attached. The solder metal has a lower melting temperature and may be aided in its flow by the use of chemical fluxes. Common solders are based on the metals, lead, tin, and silver.

Welding is the name applied to the process of fusing two pieces of the same metal together. This is done by bringing both pieces to their melting point and allowing them to flow together. Often a rod composed of the same metal is used for filler to prevent depressions in the finished joint and to fill separations. The examples shown in Fig. 43 demonstrate the effect of this process on the expressive outcome of the welded work. Welding may also refer to the hammering of two pieces of metal until they combine in a permanent bond. This practice is much older than heat welding and dates to the pre-Christian era.

Contemporary sculptors may utilize chemical bonds and/or heat fusion when working with plastic construction. Certain chemical

Figure 41.   Leonard Cave laminate. Courtesy William Stukey.

eighty-eight

Figure 42.   Kenneth Campbell marble. Courtesy William Stukey.

Figure 43. Close-up of "Fountain" texture by Yar Chomicky. Photograph by William Bradley.

ninety

solutions act as quick solvent-fluxes which literally "weld" the individual pieces of plastic together. Plastics melt at temperatures substantially lower than those of the most common metals used for welding; thus heat fusion with certain plastics, although possible, requires a great deal of skill.

Modeling is often done on a supporting frame or skeleton structure called an *armature.* For smaller work, the armature is often no more than twisted wire which helps to support the weight of the modeling material. Wooden cross pieces are often attached by flexible wire to the main armature to help prevent the slumping of the modeling material. Such an armature is shown in Fig. 44. Larger armatures are often constructed with pipes, wood, rods, and other available material. The primary purpose of the armature is to provide support for the model, since the plastic materials are apt to slump before the model is completed. Sometimes the artist utilizes whatever materials might be available to construct an armature. Fillers of styrofoam, cans, rope, and other materials which can lighten heavy sections have been used. Picasso appropriately incorporated tin cans into the belly section of his humorous goat, a bronze casting done around 1935.

Modeling is usually done in conjunction with mold making and casting. But there are many instances where the modeled work is intended as the finished work of art. Because clay shrinks when it is heated to its fusing point, an armature to help support the clay must either burn out or melt out at a very low temperature, or the clay model must be able to support itself without the armature.

Many sculptors in the past have chosen clay as a modeling material; because it does not resist manipulation, they feel that the intimate relationship of man and material allows a great deal of expressive freedom. The modeled figures of Rodin and Degas shown in Fig. 37 and 38 attest to this intimacy.

A mold or negative receptacle must be obtained from a modeled work if the artist intends to substitute another material for the clay, wax, or plaster.

Casting Procedures. The mold made from the modeled sculpture described in the previous section can be poured direct with

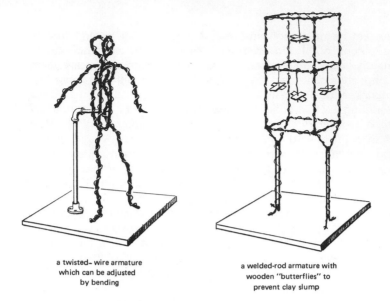

a twisted-wire armature
which can be adjusted
by bending

a welded-rod armature with
wooden "butterflies" to
prevent clay slump

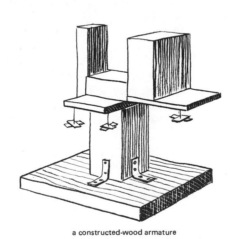

a constructed-wood armature

Figure 44.   Various armatures for clay modeling.

ninety-two

certain materials or it can serve as a receiving mold for a shell or hollow casting. In some instances, the model and mold are small enough to justify solid castings; in these cases, the mold is prepared by sealing the interior and soaking the mold in water before casting. The mold is then tied together with strong cord or wire, and all outside seams are sealed with moist clay to prevent seepage from the mold separations. The mold is inverted, held secure, and filled with the desired material. Should the mold be too large or should the artist decide against a solid casting, the mold is prepared in the same way, but alternate layers of casting material and a mesh such as burlap are applied until the desired thickness is achieved. Sometimes a flexible wax is melted and painted on the interior until a thickness of about ¼″ to ⁵⁄₁₆″ is achieved. This hollow shell of wax is then removed and prepared for metal casting.

To cast in metal requires more preparation, since there are many more factors with which to deal. In the first place, metal casting deals with molten metal at high temperatures. The safety factors here are more critical. Secondly, high temperatures generate sudden gases and shock within the mold; thus some preparation is necessary to be able to control these conditions. Several metals are cast into molds, but for our purposes we shall discuss the relatively low-melting alloy called bronze. Its melting temperature is around 1900°F, more or less depending upon its constituent metals and their proportions, and it is poured at roughly 2100°F. Historically it has been an important alloy in sculpture, and its early use as a casting material dates to at least 2500 b.c.

Channels for the bronze to enter the casting (called sprues) are carefully planned to allow the bronze to flow efficiently from the cup to the bottom of the casting (see Fig. 45). Back feeders are placed at strategic points to provide for a continued flow, and the air vents are placed to allow the hot air and gases to escape rapidly. The sprued wax model is then soaped and imbedded in investment. The wax is removed by placing the entire investment in a large oven called a kiln, where it is slowly heated to a temperature high enough to remove the wax and to decalcinate (drive out the chemical water) from the investment. The result of the burnout is an investment with a hollow interior the shape of the wax. The core investment is held securely in place by the chaplets shown in Fig. 45. The bronze is then poured into the hollow cup and the interior cavity is quickly filled with molten material. This process is referred to as the *cire perdue* or lost-wax process.

Other methods of wax casting include working directly on a core and working directly with wax rather than clay.

Bronze casting is also accomplished with sand molds. For this procedure a positive model is required, usually of plaster or wood, which is placed in a flask. The model is then rammed with oiled or wet sand and clay until the solid packing of the sand produces a single piece of the mold. The flask with the imbedded model is inverted so that the other side of the model is exposed. The second half of the sand mold is rammed into the flask. The mold is opened and the original model is carefully removed, leaving a negative mold or hollow area in the packed sand. The component parts of a sand mold are illustrated in Fig. 46. Sometimes the sand is baked in an oven before pouring—whether or not depends upon the binder that is used. Both honey and molasses have been used for binders in sand molds.

Painting

Painting has been used by people in a greater variety of ways than any of the other categories we are discussing, and this very flexibility represents one of the distinctive aspects of the medium. It has been used on boards, papers, canvas, walls, ceilings, and exteriors. This flexibility seems to be a logical outgrowth of the varieties of suspensions or media within which pigment is ground. In the discussion of drawing we learned about the combination of mineral pigments with both wax and oil. Those drawing materials come quite close to a reasonable definition for painting materials, except for the degree to which both wax and oil are used. The inks also could be described as painting material—especially the colored ink currently available for artists' use. We may consider the colored

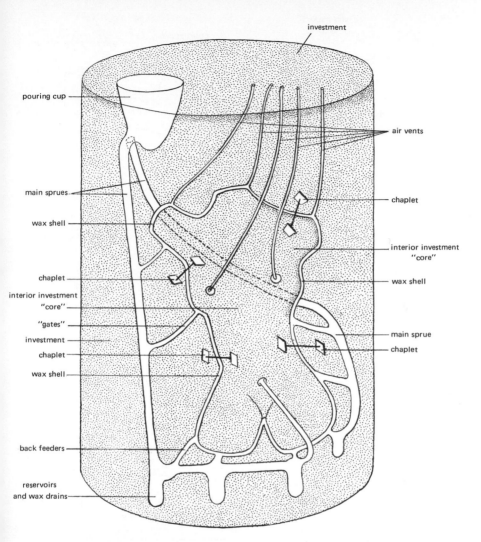

investment

pouring cup

air vents

main sprues

chaplet

wax shell

interior investment "core"

chaplet

wax shell

interior investment "core"

main sprue

"gates"

chaplet

investment

chaplet

wax shell

back feeders

reservoirs and wax drains

Figure 45. Lost-wax investment showing core chaplets and sprueing. This method is often used for small bronzes.

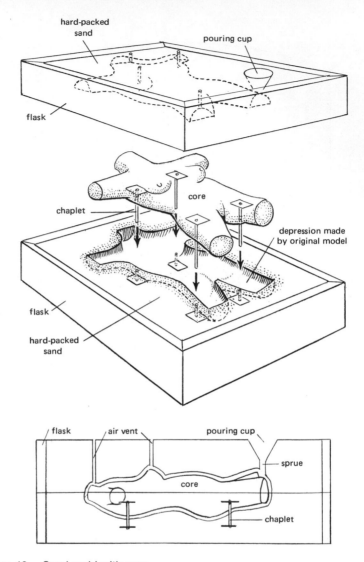

Figure 46. Sand mold with core.

inks used by Egyptian artists in the Middle and New Kingdoms as representative of the earliest examples of painting as we know it today. Much of this very early work was done with water-based inks or stains directly on plaster (in the tomb interiors) or on prepared glued walls or wood surfaces. During the New Kingdom a system was apparently developed whereby artists could employ beeswax in their painting. This advance allowed for more desirable and more intense colors. The history of painting from that time on has been marked by a concern for the quality of the suspension into which the pigment is ground. Some of the more desirable suspensions have been those which allow for brilliant and rich color, do not darken readily, provide for a wide range of plasticity (from transparent washes to opaque impastos or pastes), are flexible enough to prevent cracking and scaling, and would provide a variety of working or drying times. An equally intensive interest developed which should be noticed here: the surface material upon which the paint is to be placed and the preparation of that surface has become inextricably tied to the painting media, since certain combinations do not last long and deteriorate because of an inharmonious relationship between them. Aside from the material aspects of painting, which will be discussed in the next few pages, painting remains distinctive because of the individual artist's exploitation of these qualities in his work. The painting by Gericault in Fig. 7 contrasts strongly in both texture and the use of glazes (transparent oil washes of color which produce the depth of surface characteristics of this technique) with the painting by van Gogh in Fig. 9. Van Gogh used a heavy impasto to develop a surface texture which literally provides shadows in a sculptural or three-dimensional way. Some artists, including Franz Hals and Rembrandt van Rijn, utilized both techniques in the same painting. Contemporary painters have the added advantage of using materials which "set up" or dry chemically, such as the acrylics and related polymers. In a relatively short period of time an impasto painting can be developed and dryed with these materials.

Painting techniques may be categorized in several ways to describe their expressive characteristics, but perhaps a most fruitful direction for us would be to describe painting in terms of the media or suspensions which hold the pigment. In this way we shall be able to describe the preparation required of each surface and the distinctive features of each of the media or suspensions used. Pigments for painting are ground into many suspensions, but the ones described here are the most common of these: the water-bound pigments (fresco and fresco secco), the wax-bound pigments (encaustics), the emulsion-bound pigments (temperas) the oil-bound pigments, and the plastic-bound pigments.

Fresco and Fresco Secco. From earliest evidence it appears that painting began with fresco secco work on walls and panels and somewhat later was expanded by the invention of true fresco painting and encaustics. The primary distinction between the true fresco, or *buon fresco,* and fresco secco, or *distemper*, is that the true fresco is done with pigments in a water solution on a ground of wet lime plaster, whereas the fresco secco procedure is to paint with water-suspended pigments or certain of the emulsion-suspended pigments on dry plaster. *Buon fresco* is considered to be one of the more difficult of the painting procedures, since it requires the artist to lay up a wall in small enough sections to permit time to apply the pigment before the plaster sets up (dries). As the individual sections are built up, slight changes in the consistency of the lime plaster or the intensity of the pigment can occur. The fresco artist must take great care in blending the edges of the individual sections. Still, it is not possible to eliminate all traces of the separation. The resulting joints between the sections of lime plaster are called *intonaco joints.* In some early frescoes these irregular patchlike sections are clearly visible. The intonaco itself is the final smooth coating on a previously prepared surface. The artist applies to the wall as large a section of the intonaco as he feels he can complete in one working period. He begins immediately to paint with his water-bound pigments so that the colors themselves impregnate the intonaco layer. In this way the medium and the ground (surface preparation) unite to form very durable paintings. One of the characteristic features of the fresco is its limited color range, since most pigments combine readily with lime to produce muted colors. A second distinctive quality of the fresco is its mat or dull surface. It can easily be viewed from many angles without interference from reflected light. Buon fresco and fresco secco paintings were done primarily for the interior and exterior decoration of architectural structures and houses. It is important to realize this, since we see them in an entirely different way when they have been reduced in size for book reproduction. Frescoes have seldom, if ever, been intended as small-scale, intimate paintings, but instead (like stained glass windows) to command large areas.

Fresco secco is a contradiction in terms, since fresh (*fresco*) and dry (*secco*) are apparently inconsistent. If we can view the terms to mean that the water-bound pigment or emulsion pigment is "fresh" and used on a "dry" lime-plaster surface, however, we may be able to remember the difference between these two terms more readily.

Early plaster painting in Egyptian tombs during the late dynasties (New Kingdom, c. 1300 B.C.) were oftentimes simply watercolor or water-bound pigments applied directly to dry plaster (distemper painting). Because of the arid climate and the fact that the tombs in which such painting was done were carefully sealed from the inside, the paintings were protected from scaling and flaking off. Later paintings, such as those done as murals for Roman buildings (c. A.D. 250) and the wall and ceiling paintings of Renaissance Europe, required some resolution of the moisture problem. It was the development of true fresco (buon fresco) which solved the problem of paint layers scaling from walls, and the development of new preparations of panels, walls, and emulsion pigments which solved the moisture problem for tempera painting.

Encaustic Painting. The binder used in encaustic painting was often pure beeswax. Later, other waxes and wax blends were developed. The colors are mixed hot and applied in a paste to liquid state. It is believed that early users of this process maintained a cradle or small container of hot coals which was passed closely over the surface of the painting to burn in the colors and to help blend them. Some excellent examples of this process have survived from as early as the pre-Christian era in Rome. The surface upon which encaustic painting was accomplished was usually wood paneling.

***Emulsion Suspensions* (the Temperas).** This group of painting media were originally represented by a single emulsifier—whole hen's egg and water—into which the pigment was ground. Egg acts as a glue as well as a siccative (drier). The oils from the egg mix easily with water when they are both in liquid form, but the resulting paint "skin" is waterproof. Many more emulsifying agents have been used, among them casein, glue, gum, and egg with sun-thickened oils.

The caseins are products of milk. The specific ingredient is called caseinogen, which is a white amorphous phosphoprotein most evident in curdled-milk products. The earliest painting caseins were made from finely ground cheese, but other milk products and milk itself have since become regular sources. When this white material protein is combined with an alkali it produces a very durable hornlike plastic called paracasein, the same substance produced naturally by horned, hoofed, and antlered animals. This glutenous characteristic provides an effective emulsifier-glue within which to grind pigments. Casein preparations are also used in conjunction with pure gypsum or plaster of paris to provide a liquid surfacing material or ground for preparing a board or canvas painting. This mixture is referred to as *gesso* (pronounced "jesso"). Many pre-Renaissance paintings done on panel were prepared with casein-plaster ground and painted with egg-tempera suspensions.

Among the glue suspensions, caseins have remained the most popular, although as a surface preparation gesso is not as well adapted to canvas preparation as the animal glues. A popular canvas preparation which has remained essentially unchanged over several centuries is a liquid glue prepared from boiled rabbit skins. On the other hand, the availability of gesso has made it a popular canvas preparation also.

Originally, the pigments for egg tempera were obtained by grinding gemstones such as azurite, lapis lazuli, hematite, malachite, and using rare metals such as silver and gold. The artist used his medium to provide a means by which he could exploit the qualities of the gemstones themselves. This required great patience and skill and was related to the philosophy that these rare or precious materials were in and of themselves majestic. On occasion a commission painting would specify the exact amounts of each precious mineral to be used in a painting, but as the concern for color clarity and range finally took precedence the use of precious minerals and metals declined.

A variation of egg-tempera emulsion utilizes other specially refined oils, such as sun-thickened poppyseed oil. In this case the dry pigment powder is mixed in the egg-oil emulsion in the painting studio.

Another kind of tempera medium (although seldom referred to as "tempera") is comprised of gum solution, water, and pigment. It is called *watercolor.* Usually the pigment is in a moist form packaged in tubes, but it is also available in cake form. The uniqueness of this tempera is its transparency, which allows white surfaces to show through and brighten the applied paint. It is readily soluble in water and is capable of a wide spectrum of concentrated pigment from tinted water to near-opacity. Zinc white or powdered chalk can be added to transparent watercolor to produce an opaque medium referred to as *gouache.* The temperas currently sold commercially as poster paint, school tempera, and the like are generally a gum-based *gouache.* All of the temperas are soluble in water and could technically be called watercolors.

We have already discussed the very old practice of combining melted beeswax with pigment in the process known as *encaustic,* but the beginning of oil painting—where various mixtures of oil were used as binders—came much later. Our earliest examples of major work done with oil-based paints seem to be centered around an artist known only as the "Master of Flemalle" (c. 1425) and the excellent painter Jan Van Eyck (1390–1441), although there is still much controversy about where and by whom oil painting began. When the oil paintings are compared with the earlier panel paintings done in tempera alone, one is immediately struck with both the transparency of the surface and the clarity and range of color in the oils. These distinctive qualities, coupled with the fact that properly primed canvases painted with prepared oils do not appreciably change during drying time, has made oil painting the one most popular medium in the arts since around A.D. 1600. Many people equate the term *art* with oil painting because of its popularity even today.

The most common binder in oil painting is linseed oil. This oil is made from the seed of the flax or linum, that magnificent plant whose straw makes the linen canvas and whose oils bind the pigments to itself. Other mixtures of various oils are used to provide transparency or to speed drying. Once dry, these oil binders produce a tough and durable skin. Quite complex mixtures of transparent oil binders for *glazes,* or oil washes, are often prepared. When oil painting was first introduced in the fifteenth century, it was most often combined with egg-tempera painting and done on wood panels. The general use of oil paints prepared by individual artists and applied to canvas surfaces stretched over wooden frames as we know it today did not actually begin until after the end of the High Renaissance.

Heavy impasto build-up of paint on the surface of a painting was unique to oil painting until the invention of the new plastic-based pigments. The artist using oils is free to develop lines or edges directly in his work to emphasize a color, plane, or texture.

The flexibility of oil paint with regard to color and clarity and the qualities of impasto and transparency account for a good deal of the popularity of oils, but these paints did not become the panacea for all of the painter's ills. The artist who uses oil paint must exercise several cautions, since oil paint did not prove to be as color-fast or as durable as fresco, encaustic, and egg-tempera. Chipping, flaking, cracking, and peeling are problems most often associated with oil paint. In addition, the pigments suspended in oil often darken in time.

Plastic-bound pigments are formulated by a pigment-impregnated liquid (paste) polymers. They can be mixed with water to produce "washes" or can be used directly in paste form without the cracking and shrinkage problems associated with oil-based pigments. These paints are also "waterproof" when they dry, a quality which makes them particularly suitable for "supergraphics," as in the painting of an entire side of a multistory building.

Graphics

When the stone carver and the painter put their hands to their work, they most often produce a single instance of a work or a single unique object for viewing. What we see is a one-of-a-kind work characteristic of the material from which it was made, of the artist who made it, and perhaps of the times during which it was made. These works are gradually produced by taking away material in a systematic way or by adding material until it is completed.

The *print,* on the other hand, is characteristically different from these methods. It is a work of art produced by a duplicating procedure. The types of prints discussed in this section include those produced by 1) relief surfaces, where ink placed on the highest plane is transferred (such as in woodcuts), 2) intaglio surfaces, where ink is forced into recessed lines and transferred under pressure (such as in engraving), and 3) planographic surfaces where ink is transferred from a single plane (such as in lithography). When we see a print we are not viewing a unique instance of the work. The print is only one of several copies of the artist's plate. The artist has not put his hand to the work that we see. Nor has the object we see been gradually constructed. It was printed in one operation (or one series of operations) and is actually a mirror image of the original work. The primary difference between the printmaking processes and the direct processes is that in printmaking a mechanical procedure separates the artist from the product. The artist in this case prepares an object which will, by means of a mechanical process, produce a work of art.

The artist who chooses to work with the mechanical procedure of printmaking must interpret all ideas in terms of the process he has chosen, and consequently our appreciation of his work must be grounded to some extent in the understanding of these processes themselves. The categories commonly used are inclusive enough for our purposes here. They are predicated upon the principle that ink can be preserved on three planes: a raised plane, a lowered plane, or a flat plane. The terms used to describe these categories are *relief* (printing from a raised line), *intaglio* (printing from a lowered line), and *planographic* (printing from the same plane as the ground). Each of these procedures maintains unique characteristics which we can discuss.

The printmaker's intention is somewhat different from other artists', since he begins with a plan to produce several duplicates of his work (an *edition*). Sometimes the edition is small, but other times many impressions of the plate are made. The artist usually signs each print and provides us with a pair of numbers which tell us the print's order in the sequence of production and the total number of impressions taken. As an example, the notation "6/14" tells us that we are viewing the sixth out of a total of fourteen impressions. This notation, which guarantees the print's integrity, is a convention among artists.

Printmaking grew out of a search for an inexpensive way of distributing religious pictures and for advertising the fairs in medieval Europe. Many of these early works (referred to as *incunabula*) were in the form of playing cards, and were apparently sold as souvenirs to the travelers who attended the fairs. Today, multiple printing has now given way to large-volume reproduction. Such reproduction is usually photographically accomplished in editions of thousands.

There are many materials, tools, and processes used in the production of prints, despite the fact that they all have certain characteristics in common. Firstly, printing involves the transference of ink from the artist's work to another surface. With two exceptions (the stencil and the photograph), ink is applied to one surface and the two surfaces are brought together under pressure. Secondly, the "print" (the surface to which the ink is transfered), is always the reverse of the original plate. The printmaker is concerned with this fact, since reversing a design will often affect its aesthetic appeal and compositional integrity. The various processes used to accomplish printmaking represent different kinds of control over the line, value, and texture of the work. A wood block, for example, does not allow the flexibility of line and value found in the etching process because of the resistance of the material; lithography, on the other hand, provides even more flexibility. Rooted in the printmaking processes is the attempt to find control over certain desirable characteristics. And even though primary control seems to be that exercised over the areas which will print and the areas which will not, value, texture, and line character are controlled as much by the processes themselves.

In the *relief process* ink is placed only on the raised areas of the block. Consequently, the line control is quite different from that used in *intaglio printing,* where the ink is forced into the lowered areas and wiped away from the raised surface. To carve "around" a line is somewhat more difficult than to carve "out" a line from a surface. The characteristic difference in freedom between these two types of lines is clearly demonstrated when we view the relief woodcut by Albrecht Durer (Fig. 47) and compare it to the intaglio engraving by Martin Schongauer (Fig. 48). In the woodcut the raised surface of the block produced the image for transfer, but in the engraving the lines which were cut down into the plate held the ink and produced the images for transfer. Woodcuts are characteristically more restrictive and bold. Engraving provides the artist with greater flexibility and control over lines, values, and textures. "Wood engraving," however, does not always refer to recession of the line, but often means that white ink was used and printed on black paper.

Another intaglio process is called *etching.* Aside from the technical differences in formulation procedures, etching has its own distinctive properties. The line which results from an etched plate seems freer and less restrictive than either the woodcut or the engraving, since very little effort is needed to produce a line in the etching process (see Fig. 49). The procedure for preparing a plate for etching is not complicated, but at root it determines the freedom with which the artist can work. A metal plate is covered with an

Figure 47. Albrecht Dürer, *The Apocalypse: The Four Horsemen*, woodcut. Rosenwald Collection, National Gallery of Art.

Figure 48. Martin Schongauer, *The Nativity* (c. 1480–90), engraving. Rosen-wald Collection, National Gallery of Art.

Figure 49. Rembrandt, *Christ Preaching*, etching. Bequest of Mrs. H.O. Havemeyer, 1929, The Metropolitan Museum of Art.

acid-resistant material—basically wax—and the lines are easily drawn through the wax to expose the metal plate. An acid bath is then used to etch the lines into the plate. These procedures will be discussed later on when we explore each of the intaglio and relief processes in depth. Suffice it to say here that the chief characteristic difference between these processes is most evident in the nature of the control over the material itself.

Another general category of printmaking is called *planography,* in which the printing surface is not achieved by cutting the background or the foreground into the block or plate, but by treating the surface of the printing block. *Lithography,* the most sophisticated and widely used process of this group, is based primarily on the fact that oil and water do not mix. Therefore, when a wax pencil is drawn across the printing block (usually a rectangular piece of polished limestone) and then flooded with glycerine water, the artist rolls oil-based ink across the stone and the ink is deposited only on the wax pencil lines. This procedure allows the artist to work directly on the stone in as free and direct a way as drawing with pencil or crayon on paper. The lithograph requires less pressure than the intaglio process, and consequently the appearance of the transferred image is somewhat distinctive. The pressure mark on the paper is quite pronounced in intaglio processes but not noticeable on the lithographic print.

We can judge to some degree the nature of the process by which prints were accomplished by studying the characteristics of the lines. The *woodcut* line is studied, bolder, wider, and seems to delineate or separate the cut-out areas. There is little attempt to use the line itself as the expressive component, and the attention that the artist gives to the areas that he removes become quite apparent. In the *engraving* the line is used as an expressive component and the negative or background areas are consciously much less important. The line becomes more delicate and curvilinear. In the *etching* process the line character is influenced by the fact that the artist is not as limited by the resistance of material. His linear development is nearly as free of resistance as the artist who draws on paper. Still, the ultimate control over line in printmaking is in the lithograph, where the resistance to linear control is virtually the same as in drawing, for the marks are produced by drawing directly on the stone.

In all of these processes, prints made from the same plate are distinctive as a group in that they each have the same characteristic pressure marks and contain the same inking irregularities. Also, each is part of a group or *edition* which sets it apart from the usual one-of-a-kind definition. Further, each is the reverse of the original design accomplished by the transfer of ink from plate to paper.

Other Graphic Processes. There are some other printing procedures which do not quite meet the criterion for printing we have set. Stenciling, masking, screening, and photography all provide for duplication by means of mechanical intervention, but the ink is not transferred from one surface to the other, and, although pressure is used to accomplish the "print," there is no distinct impression left on the final product. Photography, of course, does not involve ink or pressure but does deal with both negative and positive reversal techniques. Of this group the silk-screen print is most common. Upon close observation we can see the texture of the silk in the ink print. These processes are not as widely accepted in printmaking as the ones with longer histories. But in the world of advertising, silk-screening and various stenciling procedures are quite popular. Silk-screening as an art form is referred to as *serigraphy,* and often involves many colors. The serigraph in Fig. 50 demonstrates one artist's exploration of this process for expressive purposes.

Printmaking Processes. Processes in printmaking are each distinctive in their capacity to elicit an aesthetic response from the viewer. We should, therefore, discuss each of the processes along with their distinctive and expressive qualities.

In the *relief processes* prints are made from the areas left after certain background areas of the design have been cut away. Characteristic of this process is the *woodcut.* Woodcuts are generally made from even-grained wood with the grain running parallel to the carving surface. The wood block is usually cut to a thickness

Figure 50.   David Hickman, *Bouquet* (1964), American.

of a little under one inch. Typical woodcut blocks have been made from pear, apple, cherry, and other fruit woods. When heavy grain is desired, a pine block is sometimes used.

The tools for the woodcut are generally the knife, the veiner, and the gouge. The knife is used to provide very fine lines and to facilitate the removal of heavier V-shaped sections of the block. Veiners and gouges provide an even method for removing material and/or producing heavier lines in the block (Fig. 51).

In this relief process the wood is cut or gouged until only the intended design remains in relief on the surface. The block is inked in such a manner as to assure an even coating over all the raised surfaces. Even coatings are the rule in relief printing although the beautiful multivalued ink prints of Japanese origin exploited the possibilities of graduated inking. The inking is usually done with a brayer (roller) which rolls the ink over the surface. Another inking procedure is to use a dabber made of cloth stretched over a firm support.

The ink used in printing is very thick and tacky. It is often made of pure carbon black and quick-drying linseed oil. To provide for uniform inking the printmaker first smears or rolls the ink out onto a nonporous flat surface, and after achieving a uniform coating, transfers this ink to the raised surfaces of the printing block using the brayer. Relief prints are made by placing a slightly damp piece of paper onto the inked surface of the block, backing the paper with a cardboard, and firmly rubbing the cardboard with a spoon or rounded tool. Often, the cardboard is eliminated.

Colored woodcuts are traditionally produced by cutting a separate block for each color. Opaque colorings are carefully registered so that the edge of one color fits nicely against the others. In transparent colorings, however, the artist sometimes plans for the effects produced by overlapping colors.

Wood engraving differs from the woodcut in both the utilization of materials and tools and the aesthetic outcome. The end grain is used, allowing freedom to move in all directions on the block. The block is usually brought to a fine finish before the cutting begins. Maple is a common wood used for this process, since the elimination of the "grain" is desirable.

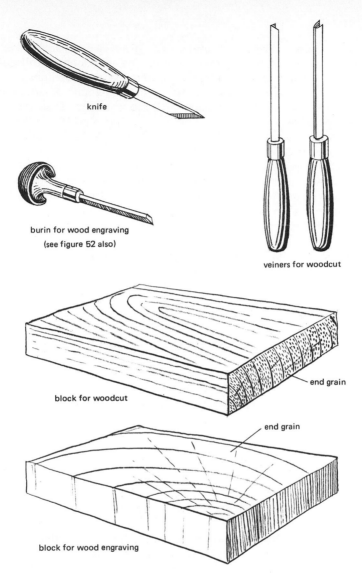

knife

burin for wood engraving
(see figure 52 also)

veiners for woodcut

block for woodcut

end grain

end grain

block for wood engraving

Figure 51.   Woodcut and wood-engraving tools.

The tools used for cutting end-grain wood are made for achieving different effects from those of the woodcut. Fine lines are easier to achieve in wood engraving, and the development of value gradations through the use of texturing tools and fine-line tools is common. The wood engraver uses the same tools as the metal engraver—burins or gravers. Wood engraving also differs from the woodcut in that white ink is often printed on a black surface.

Other relief processes which are of more recent origin but nevertheless extend the possibilities and qualities possible with relief printing are linoleum printing, metal relief printing, and collographic printing. The *linoleum* print is achieved much like the woodcut, since it is carved from a linoleum-faced wood block. Linoleum is a much less resistant material than wood, and thus provides greater freedom of movement in all directions. *Metal relief* is usually accomplished in soft metal plates by utilizing either the burin (graver) or by etching background areas into the plate. The *collograph* is produced by fastening material to a plate, inking it, then printing under pressure. None of these processes have detracted from the traditional methods of producing relief prints. Woodcuts and wood engravings seem to remain aesthetic choices.

In the *intaglio processes* the low parts of the design rather than the high parts hold the ink which is transferred to the paper. The plates for these processes are usually metal, and the lines are either cut into them with sharp tools or eaten into them with acids. The plate is heated for inking purposes, since the ink used is stiff and tacky. Rough netting or a "fat rag" is used to help distribute the ink over the surface of the plate and to wipe off surfaces which are intended to be ink free. The final wipe before printing is often done with a folded piece of tarlatan or cloth paper. When a clean wipe is used the artist often gently pulls ink up from the lines by lightly stroking them with a clean rag. This process is referred to as *retroussage*. The effect is to visually soften the otherwise hard lines. This flexibility in the intensity of ink over various parts of the plate increases the artist's control over the value structure of the print. Another factor that distinguishes the intaglio print is that, when the print is taken, a damp paper backed by a cushion is subjected to enough pressure to force the paper down into the recessed areas of the plate, where it receives the ink. The texture produced by this action is noticeable to the touch. The dried ink is often in relief on the finished print. Another characteristic pressure mark is produced by the edge of the plate. Most intaglio prints are slightly recessed into the paper. This "plate mark" is sometimes eliminated by cutting around it before matting and framing the print.

In intaglio printing the pressure gradually breaks down and wears away the edges of the cut or etched lines, a factor that limits the edition and explains why the earliest prints of an edition are generally valued more highly than the later ones.

The plates used for intaglio processes are generally copper or zinc, although steel, iron, and brass are sometimes used for engraving. The plates are of thicknesses which range between $\frac{1}{2}''$ and $\frac{1}{16}''$. They are perfectly flat and highly polished before being altered. The plate edges are often beveled, which results in a beveled "plate mark" on the finished print.

The press used for intaglio printing must be able to exert strong pressure on the plate. Ordinarily, the press has two steel rollers which are held firmly in a heavy frame. A flat steel bed moves horizontally between the rollers. Adjustable springs on the top roller enable the press to develop a very high pressure. The press is usually operated manually by turning a geared handle that activates the rollers, which pull the entire press set-up through them.

The press set-up consists of the press bed; the intaglio plate covered by a paper which is dampened (so that it will be flexible enough to be forced into the lines of the intaglio plate without tearing); a blotter to soak up water forced out by the pressure; and felt blankets to assure equal pressure over all surfaces. Each time a print is made the plate must be reinked and wiped. This process requires a great deal of skill and is most often done by the artist himself, although some artists have the actual inking and printing done by professional printers. (In some cases the artist makes the drawing only and has the entire intaglio process done, including the cutting or etching of the plate and the printing.) When the first print is run, it is drawn from the plate and inspected by the artist, who makes judgments about the inking, the structure, and the lines. This first "proof" may suggest alterations of various kinds, which are then incorporated and inspected in the second "proof" or "state." When the artist is satisfied with a "state," the edition is run. The edition numbering does not usually include the early states of the plate, but it is interesting to study the artist's proofs, since they represent a historical record of his final decision.

Recessing the line into an intaglio plate may be done in several ways; the artist often combines methods. It is not always possible for us to distinguish between the methods used. Etching and drypoint may be combined on a single plate, for instance, making it difficult for the laymen to distinguish differences or to categorize prints by these methods (etching, drypoint, engraving, etc.). It is usually better to think of the four general printmaking categories here and to identify prints as relief, intaglio, planographic, or stenciled. After we make such distinctions, it is easier to identify the technical methods employed.

In the *drypoint* process, a very sharp point is used to scratch the line into the metal plate (usually soft copper). A deposit of metal develops along the line in the form of a *burr.* If the burr remains during inking and printing, the line produced is different from those in other types of engraving, since the ink is captured in and around the burr of the line, producing a fuzzy, soft line. The skilled printmaker can exploit such lines for his expressive purposes, although the producible edition from such plates is quite small. As prints are taken, the burrs gradually wear down, and thus a drypoint plate with its burrs worn away is nearly the same as an engraving plate. The tool used for drypoint differs from regular engraving tools in that it does not actually remove the metal from the plate but displaces it. The lines produced by drypoint may be very fine to quite heavy, depending upon the pressure applied to the tool while engraving. Since drawing while applying pressure restricts the amount of flourish possible, drypoint lines are characteristically more restrained than either engraving or etching. Another characteristic of the drypoint process is the resultant value structure, since the drypoint plate cannot be wiped as thoroughly as other intaglio plates. The burr on a drypoint plate may be either single or double, depending on the angle at which the pointed tool was employed.

The *mezzotint* is closely related to the drypoint process in that it also relies on a burr to hold and transfer the ink, but is better suited than drypoint for producing tints (its name means "middle tones" or "halftones"). But whereas the drypoint relies on burrs produced from a line, the Mezzotint relies on an even distribution of burrs over the entire plate. These burrs are produced by a fine toothed blade known as a "rocker." The rocker is rocked back and forth in all directions over the entire plate, producing an even texture of burrs. Since, as in drypoint, the burrs will hold ink, it follows that inking the textured plate at this time would produce a solid tone of black. To operate with this process it is thus necessary to scrape off the burrs from any part that is to be of a lighter value. Should the artist decide to develop some areas as white, then he must make sure that all of the burr produced by the rocker is eliminated. Usually, the surfaces to be white are polished after being scraped. The mezzotint process makes possible many tones of grey, which are produced by varying the amount of burr left standing on the plate.

In producing the engraving the artist does not utilize the displacement of metal to achieve results, but instead uses tools designed to eliminate the metal from the line of cut. As in drypoint, the tools are pushed along the path of the desired line. The engraving tools are called "burins" or "gravers," and come in many varieties for many functions. The chief burins used are the anglet, scorpers, tinting tools, and the lozenge (see Fig. 52). Each produces a characteristic line and helps the artist to complete the plate efficiently. The engraving tools are built in such a way that they may be used nearly parallel to the surface of the plate. As they are pushed along the plate, a fine thread of metal is removed, leaving sharp, clean lines. The plate is then usually scraped to eliminate any burr which may have been inadvertently produced. The print which results from the engraved plate has lines which are sharp and clean, characteristic of the engraving process.

Cutting the plates for engraving usually requires some kind of

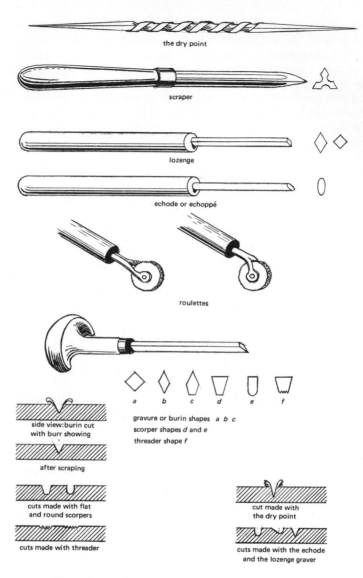

the dry point

scraper

lozenge

echode or echoppé

roulettes

side view: burin cut
with burr showing

after scraping

cuts made with flat
and round scorpers

cuts made with threader

gravure or burin shapes   *a b c*
scorper shapes *d* and *e*
threader shape *f*

a   b   c   d   e   f

cut made with
the dry point

cuts made with the echode
and the lozenge graver

Figure 52.   Engraving tools.

one hundred eighteen

support to prevent the plate from moving away from the tools. A leather pillow or "engraver's pad" is used for this purpose.

The tints produced in engraving are done in two ways. First, a tinting tool can be used to cut many close parallel lines into the surface in areas where darks are preferred. This tool is constructed in such a way that several parallel cutters operate together with one pass. The second method for producing tints on an engraving plate is by inking the plate with differing amounts of ink. During printing, this inking procedure produces tints from black to white.

Whereas lines produced on the dry-point plate are scratched by pulling the tool and the lines produced in the engraving plate are accomplished by pushing the tool, lines on the *etching* plate are drawn through a material which has very little resistance. The resulting line is much freer and more versatile.

To prepare an etching plate the artist must coat its surface with an acid-resistant material called a *ground.* The clean and polished plate is sufficiently warmed to receive a coating of the ground (a mixture of resin, wax, and pitch), which is rolled into a ball and moved over the heated plate until it melts producing an even coating. Some contemporary replacements of the "ball ground" can be applied cold, since they are combined in liquid form with highly volatile solvents. Many of these grounds are pigmented so as to provide a strong contrast with the metal and thus help the artist see where and what he is drawing. When the traditional "ball ground" is used, the plate is often blackened with carbon from a candle so that the contrast is greater. Besides the hard-ground preparation a soft-ground preparation is sometimes used. The soft ground is similar to the hard-ground composition, except that it has more tallow in it. Soft grounds do not adhere to the plate as well as hard grounds; consequently, soft-ground work permits different possibilities. One of the methods of working the soft grounds is to place a paper on the ground and to draw directly on the paper with a pencil. Wherever the pressure from the pencil touches the plate, the ground lifts, exposing the metal. An expansion of this idea is to press materials such as mesh netting, lace, or cloth against the ground, each of which produces a characteristic texture. The plate is then etched in the usual manner.

Etching needles such as the ones shown in Fig. 53 are the tools most often used for producing the lines in etching. These lines are typically much more curvilinear, since the artist is able to move with less resistance through the ground than through metal. The needles, which come in a variety of widths, are used primarily for detailed uniform lines. Used slightly less frequently but equally important to the etching craft is the "echode," an oval-shaped needle which allows the artist to vary the width of the line by rotating it. Another tool occasionally used to texture or to darken areas of the print is the "roulette," a wheel which produces fine dots or pinholes through the surface of the ground. When these dots are etched into the plate they provide reservoirs which hold the ink for transfer. All the tools used for preparing etching plates are purposefully blunted to provide ease of movement through the ground and across the metal.

When the drawing in the ground of an etching plate is complete, the sides and back of the plate are covered with acid-resistant asphaltum or shellac to prevent acid corrosion. Thus the only bare sections left on the plate are the parts exposed by drawing or stippling through the ground.

The plate with the finished drawing is submerged in a bath of acid called "mordant." The usual mordant is an admixture of dilute nitric acid and iron chloride. Nitric acid has a tendency to widen the lines by eating or "biting" both vertically down into the plate and horizontally in both directions. The iron chloride bites downward into the plate, but does not appreciably widen the line. The combination of these two acids seems most efficient and useful and, in fact, represents the formula developed in the eighteenth century called *Dutch mordant*. The acid bath must be occasionally agitated or stirred to eliminate the bubbles caused by the action of the nitric acid and to clean off the residue sediment caused by the action of the iron chloride. Experienced etchers are able to determine the depth of etch by factors such as the temperature of the acid, the length of time the plate has been in the bath, and the dilute strength of the bath.

Sometimes the plate is removed from the bath when the etched line is still shallow and fine. Such lightly etched lines hold very little

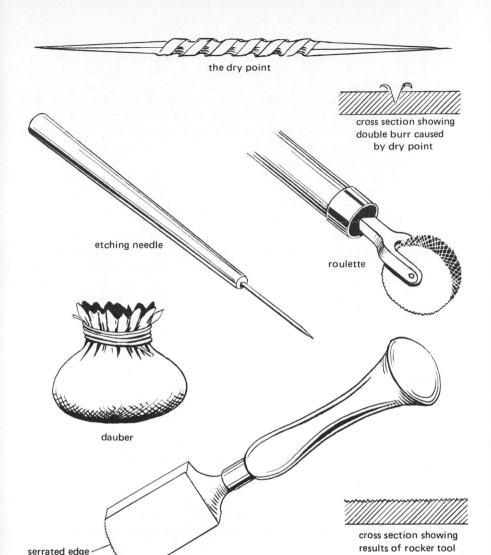

the dry point

cross section showing
double burr caused
by dry point

etching needle

roulette

dauber

serrated edge
50-100 teeth
per inch

rocker

cross section showing
results of rocker tool

Figure 53. Some etching and tinting tools.

ink, and the resulting transfer produces the lightest or faintest lines of the etching. Should the artist decide to keep these faint lines, he paints over them with stop-varnish or shellac to prevent further etching. When we look at an etched line, we can often see the varnish marks between etching baths. The plate is again placed in the mordant to continue the etching. As the lines deepen and widen they increase their capacity to hold and transfer ink. The deeper the etch the darker the line. Stop-varnish may be used several times during the etching process.

After it has been determined that the heaviest lines are sufficiently deep into the plate, the ground and varnish are removed by means of solvents and the plate is prepared for printing in the same manner as in the other intaglio processes. The first "proof" is pulled and examined. When the plate is in its original etched condition, it is referred to as the "first state," since the artist may determine that some alterations are necessary to achieve what he wants. In some instances, he may simply deepen or widen certain lines with engraving tools, or he may add lines or textures to the plate. On the other hand, it may be necessary to remove lines from the plate or redo larger areas. To do this the artist employs a scraping tool which literally scrapes the metal away until the surface of the plate is lowered to the bottom of the etched line. Since this procedure results in a cupped depression on the plate, the artist must force the metal back to the original plane by hammering carefully from the back side. Once the plane of the plate surface is again flat and the altered area is polished, it is ready for reprocessing by either engraving or etching. Subsequent trial proofs pulled from various states of the plate help the artist refine his idea.

The *aquatint* process is related to the etching process, although it is sufficiently different from it to warrant our separate consideration.

In producing the aquatint the ground is prepared by dusting powdered resin onto the plate. When the plate is heated, the resin particles melt, leaving exposed minute metal parts around each of them which would, when placed in the acid bath, develop a plate with a consistently etched tone. By carefully planning the stop-varnish application, a wide range of tints are possible. The lightest areas may be blocked out before the first etch, and subsequent applications of stop-varnish and acid bath provide the range from light to dark values.

The aquatint has some of the advantages of painting since, in the application of stop-varnish, brushstrokes often show up among the hundreds of resin particles.

Lithography is a relatively recent addition to printmaking processes invented by Aloys Senefelder around 1796. Senefelder was not an artist but a playwright, who because of poverty was seeking an effective and inexpensive way to reproduce his plays. The story associated with the accidental discovery of lithography is quaint. Senefelder's mother had called down to his laboratory to ask him to buy some groceries. Unable to locate a paper or pencil to take down the list, he wrote it on a flat piece of limestone that happened to be in his shop, using as a writing instrument a grease crayon. Later, when he cleaned the stone by scraping the grease from the surface and washing it with water, Senefelder discovered that one of the properties of the stone is its affinity to both oil and water. The oily residue of the grease crayon remained on the stone after scraping it. The fact that he had flooded the surface with a water solution and that his tiniest scrawl on the stone remained because of the natural tendency of oil to repel water led Senefelder to experiment with the inking of the stone in this condition. The experiment was highly successful. Lithography, although embellished with many refinements, continues to be based upon these two characteristics of the material: the stones (Bavarian limestone is to this day the preferred stone) have an affinity to both oil and water, and oil and water do not mix.

The stone is usually from two to four inches thick and is brought to a flat surface plane by using various grits of carborundum and/or silicon carbide. These grits are usually in the form of powder, and the degree of abrasion ranges from rough to very fine, depending on the intended surface of the stone.

There are two widely used methods of making the drawing for the stone. In either case using the grease pencil, the artist may make the drawing (in reverse) directly on the stone, or he may draw directly on paper (without reversing the design) and then transfer the drawing to the stone. In the latter process, called "transfer lithography," a specially prepared paper is used for making the drawing. The transfer is accomplished by placing the paper face down on a heated lithograph stone and running it through a press to transfer the grease lines.

After the drawing is completed the stone is moistened and "fixed" by a solution of gum arabic and dilute nitric acid. The drawing is washed from the stone with a solvent, then moistened with water and inked. It is then ready for press.

The press set-up for lithography is somewhat different from those for other printing procedures. The stone, placed face up in the press, is covered by the dampened print paper for transfer, a blotter to receive excess moisture, and a tough greased cardboard (tympan) to aid the set-up through the press (see Fig. 54).

The press is also unique. The press bed moves on a roller much like a regular press, but at the top the roller is replaced by a stationary scraper which scrapes across the tympan as it exerts pressure on the bed set-up.

Lithograph editions are often numbered in the hundreds and sometimes in the thousands, since there are no "edges" to wear away. For this reason lithographs are usually less expensive than intaglio and relief prints, unless the artist who produced them enjoys a good and established reputation.

Innovations in photography have, by means of "sensitizing" the stone and developing it, expanding some of the possibilities with this interesting and efficient print process. The lithograph may be produced using most drawing materials, including ink and water, so long as the material used contains a sufficient amount of fat or grease.

The *stencil processes* are more closely related to the planographic process than to either relief or intaglio. Stenciling is the process of forcing or spraying ink through holes in thin sheeting to produce a design. The sheeting is often of stiff, oiled paper, but in some processes thin tissue may be used. The artist may cut only

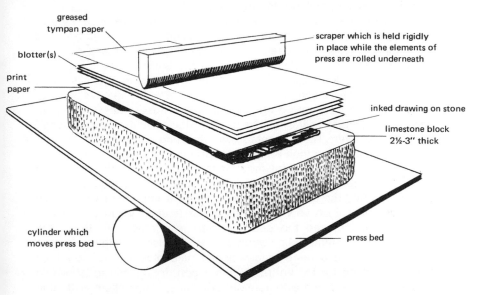

greased tympan paper

scraper which is held rigidly in place while the elements of press are rolled underneath

blotter(s)

print paper

inked drawing on stone

limestone block 2½-3" thick

cylinder which moves press bed

press bed

Figure 54.   Lithograph press elements.

holes for one color in a stencil sheet and then cut other sheets for the different colors of the design. In this case, he must carefully align or "register" each stencil sheet before printing.

The most versatile and widely used of the stencil processes in art is the silk-screen. When used as an expressive process, the result is often called a serigraph (see Fig. 50). It differs from other stenciling procedures in that it employs support membrane to hold the stencil in place and to allow for better registry. The membrane is usually of fine-mesh silk, although similar fine-mesh material is sometimes substituted. The silk screen is dampened and then stretched in a special frame with a single groove running parallel to the frame segments (see Fig. 55). The dampened screen is rolled and tamped into these grooves, which soon begin to make the silk taut. When it is dry, it is completely stretched and ready for use. Other methods of fastening the silk to the frame are somewhat less effective (stapling, tacking, taping, etc.).

Several methods of "blocking out" the screen are used. One of the most reliable and traditional is called the *glue-and-tusche* method. Tusche, an oil-based filler, is painted over the areas of the design which will eventually print. Then the entire screen is coated with a water-soluble glue. At this point all holes in the silk have been filled. The tusche is dissolved with solvents which open the areas intended for printing but leaves intact those areas which had only glue. Sometimes the tusche is water-based and shellac is used for the glue filler. The advantage in reversing these bases is that water-based inks can then be used for printing.

Another equally useful method for blocking out the screen is to gradually build up the screen with a series of tissue-paper stencils. To do this the artist usually completes a color mock-up of his finished serigraph. A very light base color is usually run before any tissue is applied, and the entire edition is printed with that base color. If, for example, six colors are to be used, ranging from a very pale blue to a deep magenta, the pale blue inking would be the initial inking for the entire edition. Upon drying, the artist would select which areas were to remain pale blue, cover them with thin tissue paper, and place the cleaned screen down over the design.

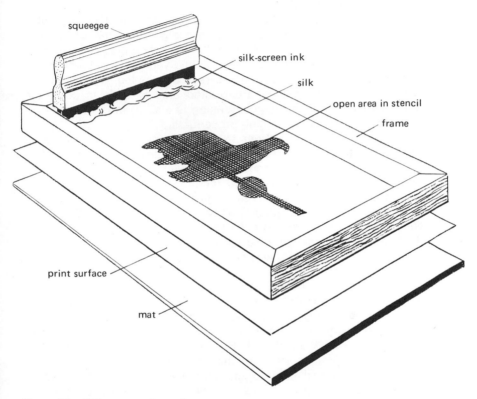

Figure 55. Silk-screen elements.

The second color is then applied. The action of the inks being forced through the screen causes the tissue stencils to adhere to the silk, permitting the rest of the edition to be run. There are many variations of both of these methods.

The printing of a silk-screen print is done with the help of a "squeegee," a rubber-tipped scraper which, when pulled across the screen, forces the gelatinous ink through the unblocked areas of the screen. It is usually possible to see the texture of the silk mesh in the finished print.

As in the other divisions of relief, intaglio, and planographic printing, photography can be used in "sensitizing" the silk screen for developing photoimages. Usually the photograph is retaken through a fine dot screen to permit subtle variations in tonality, but direct developing is also done. Direct developing produces only two values, but when they are printed side by side in color the effect is often startling. Photoscreening is also used in combination with other block-out or meshing procedures.

Photography differs from the other print processes in that it does not require the selective cutting, gouging, and scratching of material, but instead demands a selective eye to "frame" the desired elements and set the stage for the mechanical and chemical reproduction of the image. The original photography was substantially different from the photography we know today. In Beaumont Newhall's *History of Photography* he describes the first camera as a dark room, large enough for a man to enter, which had an opening in one wall. When a paper was held a short distance from the opening the entire scene from outside was reproduced and easily copied. All of this occurred in 1568 in Italy. But it wasn't until the nineteenth century that experiments in preserving the framed image by means other than hand copying were successfully carried out.

Most everyone familiar with English pottery is familiar with the name Josiah Wedgewood. But Josiah's son, Thomas, became historically important also, for his experiments with solutions of silver nitrate helped lead to the first photographic "negative."

Actually, two other men were experimenting with silver nitrate surfaces at the same time—Niepce and Daguerre in France. It was

Daguerre who perfected a reliable technique for taking photographs and preserving them. The process named by him was *daguerreotype.*

These "photographs" were not at all like those we know today. They were reverse images on a polished silvery metal plate which restricted the angles from which it could be viewed; in addition, the length of time required for exposure precluded all but still landscapes.

Recognizing the need for a "negative image" which could be reversed to produce a faithful representation, William Talbot developed both a means by which to correct reverse images and a system for developing his negative outside the camera. Later improvements included the development by Archer in 1851 of a wet colloidal solution on glass impregnated with a potassium iodide which, while still tacky, was plunged into a solution of silver nitrate and then immediately exposed to light. Preparation for the colloidon photographer was on the spot and cumbersome. It was some time before the "snapshot" was to come about.

Significant advances in photography were made in the 1880s under the strong influence of a bank clerk in Rochester, New York. George Eastman, capitalizing on the discovery (by the British physician Maddox in 1871) that gelatin could be substituted for the collodion, developed a flexible, dry film which could be rolled up and turned into position with a "turn of the key." This invention made every man a potential photographer interested in the visual composition of his own ideas. But it also stirred an angry controversy at the turn of the century between those who preferred a "pictorial art" and those who saw photography as an aesthetic engagement. Pockets of the controversy persist today, even though most university art departments, museums, and galleries seem to recognize photography as a legitimate art form (see Fig. 56).

Architecture

Aside from the peripheral considerations of architectural "gingerbread" (the use of material for exterior effect, textural combinations, wood-stone relationships, etc.) and the traditional de-

Figure 56.   A contemporary photo by Merle Cutler.

one hundred thirty

signing components which are similar to the other arts, there are some distinctions in architecture which seem to set it apart. It may be that size and the experience of enclosure account for the immediate and most obvious differences, yet function, designing for human living space, and a certain dependence on engineering developments seem to be equally important as distinctive characteristics of architecture.

Since construction and monument making have been physically the largest of the arts, it would not do to eliminate size from our discussion of architecture. From the temples and pyramids of dynastic Egypt (c. 3000 B.C.) to the World Trade Center in New York City, the exploitation of material toward size has continued. One of the earliest architectural concerns seems to have been the problems associated with enclosing large areas without the use of central columns or supporting devices. An early and magnificent solution to this problem was the Pantheon (Fig. 13), built in A.D. 118–125. In the nineteenth century the development of iron and steel girders ushered in the possibility of covering huge expanses. A second concern has been building vertically. The mythical "Tower of Babel" suggests that early civilizations were also interested in height. Prior to iron construction the culmination of efforts toward height was the Gothic cathedral (see Fig. 14), where the development of intersecting arches and buttressed walls permitted stone building to unprecedented heights. The very high buildings in New York City, Chicago, and other places began with the use of iron and steel girder construction and the now famous Parisian tower designed by Gustave Eiffel in 1889. Construction of the Eiffel Tower demonstrated the feasibility of building to great heights and led to the familiar "iron cage" construction.

Both the covering of huge expanses of land and the development of tall structures may be viewed in terms of the exploitation of the structural material available. The greatest expenditure of human and material resources have been spent in producing the structures and environments within which we live and have our being. We reside in them, they are under us, and they loom heavily above us. This much attention to enclosure must surely reflect a basic human need to control and influence environmental and social conditions.

The construction of huge buildings, although impressive and need-fulfilling, does not always result in architecture, since size and the exploitation of material only partially satisfy the definitional requirement—that is, *control.* It involves the expressive use of construction for designing living space. This means that the social functions as well as physical and personal functions are important for us to consider when we discuss architecture. The exterior and interior of an architectural structure are organized to present a particular point of view regarding functional and aesthetic space, but the point of view is often influenced by the times and conditions under which the construction took place For example, games as a human enterprise have served as the impetus for the designing of huge arenas, auditoriums, and courts, and although the structural capacity of materials has determined the design to some extent, the nature of the games and the ceremonial importance attached to them is often reflected in both the exterior and interior. Also, changing modes of religious ceremony are readily inculcated into religious architecture.

The architect has certain designing components with which to express his point of view. He may plan for a particular distribution of spaces within a space, such as the variety of rooms, areas, corridors, entries, and so on.

When we enter a building we are brought through a series of "vistas" or views which occur and change as a result of our movement through and among the entrances, rooms, and halls of the interior. These vistas are very important to our sensing of the artist's intent. We are able to experience the unfolding of a spacial design by these anticipatory glimpses of the spaces ahead of our movement. The exterior of a building, as we move around it, may be experienced in much the same way. Looking past a single plane to another gives us a particular spatial sensation. Such vistas are the telemarks of architectural experiencing. Coupled with encountering the vistas is the sensing of plane distributions. Both curved planes and geometric planes provide visual coordinates making distance and size comprehensible. When we experience an enclosure we identify its parameters and visual volume by comparing the distribution and character of the vistas and planes involved.

Ceiling heights, floor dimensions, the design and frequency of entrances, and the sequence of spaces are important aspects of the enclosure which help us to respond to an architect's point of view.

Architecture and environmental planning literally "set the stage" for human living. The Saarinen airport terminal (see Figs. 57–58) provides its transient inhabitants with a point of view regarding air travel and sets the psychological atmosphere for it. The terminal would not be nearly as effective as a religious edifice because of these psychological considerations which must go into the design of functional living spaces and the socially agreed-upon symbolization inherent in them.

Another characteristic of architecture which distinguishes it from the other arts is the factor of structural stability. The structure must meet all tests of stability if it is to survive. It would not do to have monuments, huge buildings, and tall structures collapse shortly after being erected. Structural stability limits to some degree the nature of expression. The physical properties of stone, as an example, do not permit thin walls on high structures, nor can cantilevered sections be attempted without the use of prestressed and reinforced concrete or material with similar properties. The Saarinen terminal simply could not have been built with the material available in the early 1800s. Of course, there were other reasons why such buildings were not built earlier. The societies which were developing a century ago had different architectural needs, since societal emphasis and modes of expressing the human condition were related to that particular world milieu.

Whereas the social content of architecture seems to be perpetually in evidence throughout history, the manifestations of this content are constantly changing—in part because of the developing need for new structures to house new functions (the office building, the cinema, the airport terminal, etc.) and in part because of the technological development of new structural material (structural steel, reinforced concrete, prestressed concrete, etc.). Architecture today has assumed the particularly difficult problem of environmental planning, in which buildings are integrated with and flanked by living spaces. The overarching problem in all of our major population centers today, is the provision which must be

Figure 57. Trans-World Flight Center, John F. Kennedy Airport, New York City. Photograph by Hélène Boivin.

one hundred thirty-four

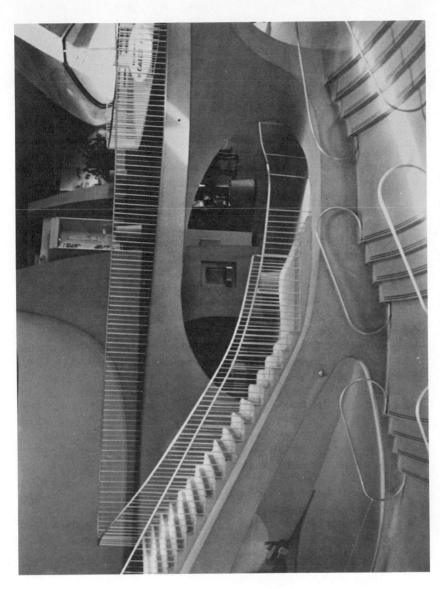

Figure 58. Trans-World Flight Center (interior), John F. Kennedy Airport, New York City. Photograph by Hélène Boivin.

made for fresh air and clean water. coupled with these survival concerns is the problem of making survival also human. To this end, environmentalists draw up plans based upon vision and history. We know, for example, that the plan for Stalingrad (now Leningrad) was superior to the design of Chicago because it provided for equal opportunity for all its citizens to be near their work, near recreational facilities, near shopping, near open country, near parks, and near the arts. Part of this plan was made possible by its linear design along the Volga River, but another part involved a deliberate provision for equating all stations in life—agronomists, factory workers, office workers, government workers, arts workers, and so forth—a realization of Karl Marx. This is a history-based view of a possibility for environmental planning. But other plans are also formulated which represent daring or visionary approaches to both environmental planning and designing for living. The layout and plan for the city of Columbia, Maryland, is such an example. Critics of the plan suggest that Columbia is merely a community of professionals, not a true city, and has therefore not solved any of the major problems of the typical city. Nonetheless, even its critics concede that Columbia is visionary and does, indeed, represent a prototype (see Fig. 59).

The linear plan of Leningrad and the "green belt" plan of Columbia would not, of course, be feasible for the huge centers of population in Moscow, Berlin, London, New York, or Los Angeles, and other designs are being considered—some as remediation proposals to alleviate current urban ills and some as entirely new cities containing communities. Until governments are willing to foot the huge bill for activating these visionary proposals, however, the only urban planning will be the small-scale, politically pork-barreled renewal programs which become incessantly vulgar theatre for ghetto box seats.

When we view architectural and environmental structures, we may sense some of the social factors which are evident in the structural design, including the relative importance our society places on certain aspects of the building or environment and our relation-

Figure 59. Town Plaza, downtown Columbia, Maryland. Courtesy The Rouse Company.

ships to them; we may sense the impulsive or expressive component in the structure as the personal use of vistas and planes are explored; and we may sense the possibilities and limitations of structural materials as they provide stability, size, and space for social and private functions.

Columns and Arches. Most of the problems encountered in construction seem to be related to strains in structures. These strains are produced by the weight and placement of material. One of the strains is caused by the direct pressure of weight on material—*compression*. The other strain is an outward thrust created when material spans two walls or supporting posts—*tension*. The history of construction has been largely concerned with these forces. thickness and height of walls, size and shape of the roof covering, weight of materials, and the open span of the interior are determined by calculated reference to these strains.

In the earliest known man-made structures, *posts* and *lintels* were used to construct dolmens (burial chambers) and *cromlechs* (religious structures) and undoubtedly many other structures for which we have no archaeological evidence. One of the early examples of the use of post and lintel for such construction is the cromlech at Stonehenge, England. Some have surmised that this particular structure was constructed according to the movement and position of the planets and stars and represents a remarkable astronomical observatory which was probably used in conjunction with an astrological view of religion. The post-and-lintel system extended into the development of predynastic Egyptian temples and later the magnificent temples in Greece, where the development of the truss and the pediment helped to distribute the roof weight outward and downward.

The stone lintels used in early construction produced tremendous strains on the posts, requiring that they be very thick or, in the case of supporting walls, that they be buttressed on the outside. In the early temples of Egypt the posts (columns) and the lintels were very massive. Sometimes columns for such structures would rise some seventy feet in the air and support lintels which spanned as much as twenty-four feet. The expanses left open beneath the lintels, however, were apparently insufficient. The great temple of the Acropolis, built in Greece some thousand years later, utilized a different technology which provided for greater spans between columns. Ictinus and Callicrates, the master architects for the Parthenon, determined that the use of wood lintels and the equilateral *truss* could open up much greater floor areas than the heavier stone allowed, and the interior colonnades were made from much thinner marble columns. In consequence, the interior chamber, called the "cella," was considerably more open than the Egyptian temples had been. With this new exploration of material came systems or "orders" of proportion. These "orders" have been arbitrarily assigned certain decorative and proportional styles which have come to be known as Doric, Ionic, and Corinthian (Fig. 60). The *Doric* temple was essentially stone throughout, smaller and more compact than the Ionic or the Corinthian. Its columns were severe, standing directly on the uppermost step of the temple (the stylobate) and rather pristine in its approach to the roof support (the entablature). The *Ionic* temple designers inculcated wood into the roof structure, varied the sizes of the columns, and changed the proportional relationships between colonnades. This new-found freedom was reflected in the design of the column base, as it approached the stylobate, and in the entablature.

The *Corinthian* design is sometimes referred to as an elaboration of the Ionic, since its chief differences seem related to column styles rather than to proportional innovation. The familiar bell-shaped capital enveloped with acanthus leaves is Corinthian.

The post-and-lintel system has always been a part of architectural engineering, and is perhaps the predominant device used in contemporary construction. Most major architectural works utilize the so-called Chicago construction, which is a slightly modified version of post-and-lintel construction in which a steel cage of posts and girders support the attached skin of glass, plastic, stone, brick, or concrete. Roof supports today seem strongly related to the truss or distributive support systems.

The *arch* is based upon a principle of graduated compression. Tension is reduced as the roof weight is gradually transformed into

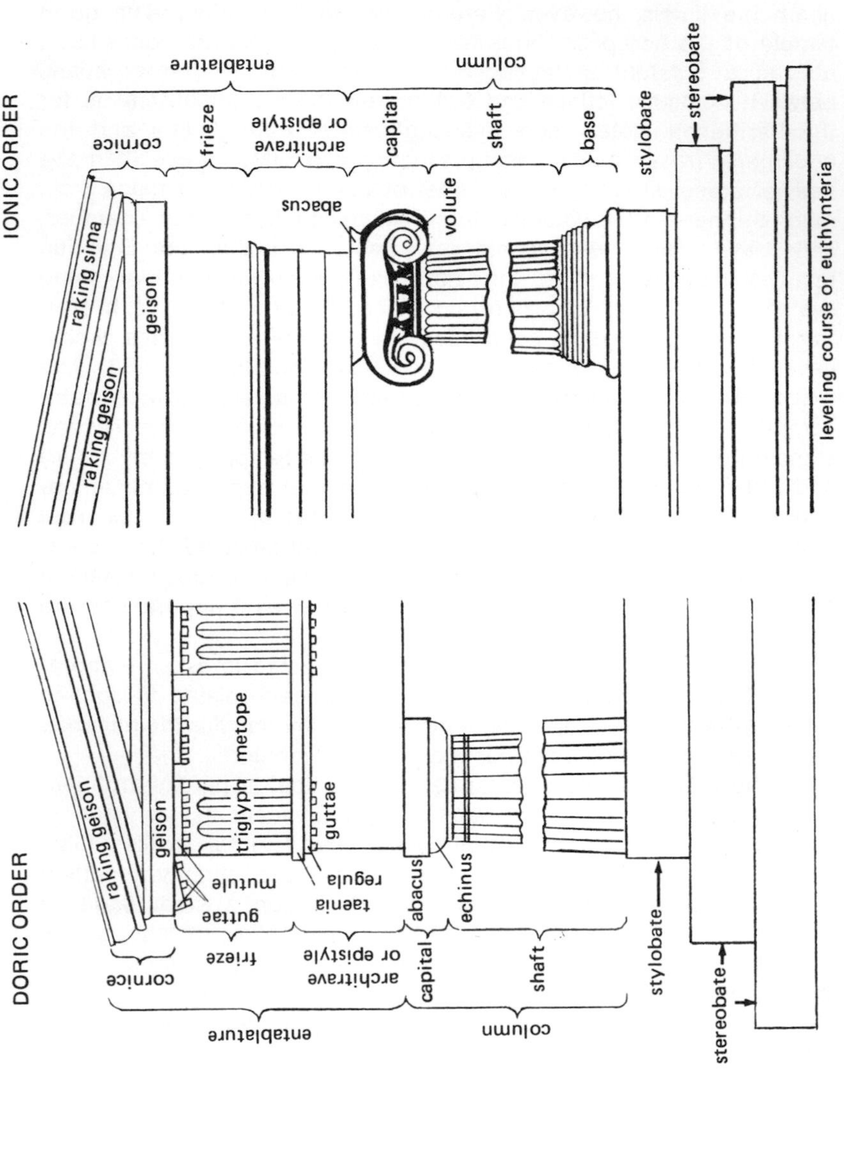

Figure 60. The Doric and Ionic orders (after Grinnell).

a compressive force. Many varieties of the arch have been developed, but generally they are made by applying similar rules of construction. On top of the columns which support the arch are "springer" stones, flat on the underside and cut to an angle on the upperside to accommodate the beveled "voussoirs." At the top of the arch is a "capstone" or "keystone" which, when placed, holds all of the supporting voussoirs in place.

During construction, an interior armature is built to hold the arch stones in place until the keystone is in position. This armature is called the "centering." Two groups of arches have generally been used in architecture. First is the *corbeled arch,* which is best illustrated when we think of carving an arch in an already constructed stone wall (Fig. 61). This arch cannot be called a true arch, since it only partially transforms tension into compression. The second group of arches are referred to as *round arches.* With these arches there is much less tension because the voussoirs have gradually transformed that strain into a downward compressive force. Round arches get their name from the original semicircle (an exact half-circle) they form from the center between the top of the two supporting posts, but many round arches have been constructed which do not conform to the geometry of the circle. Gothic arching was a version of the round arch, but because of the use of the pointed crown it expanded the height of the arches without increasing the distance between the posts. Hence the tall arches used on the Gothic cathedral permitted an elongated rectangle support (Fig. 62).

The Dome and the Vault. Arches can be continuous and used to cover large areas. If a series of round arches are distributed in such a way that they intersect at a central point on top and rest on equally spaced positions around a circle, the result is a *dome.* The advantages of a dome are related to the fact that intersecting round arches are very strong and can support a roof covering over very large open areas. When domes are used in buildings it is often necessary to support them on a rectangular base; in such cases the spaces left between the circumference of the domebase and the corner of the square upon which it sat required a stone fill

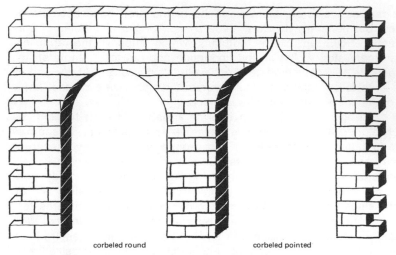

corbeled round   corbeled pointed

corbeled arches—untrue arches (the weight is distributed downward but not outward)

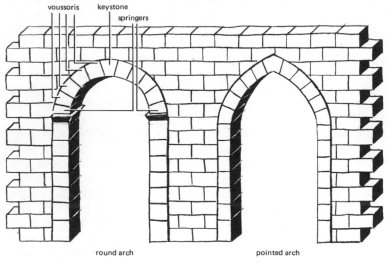

voussoris   keystone

springers

round arch   pointed arch

the round and pointed arch— true arches (the weight of the keystone load is distributed outward and downward)

Figure 61.   Corbeled arches; true arches.

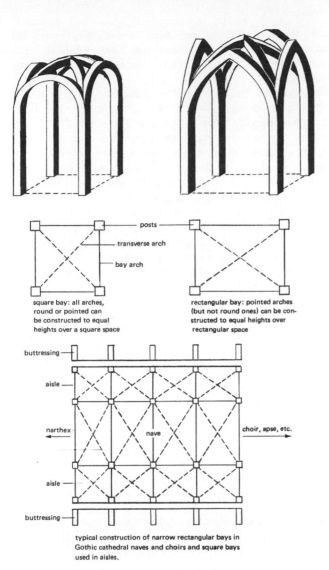

posts

transverse arch

bay arch

square bay: all arches, round or pointed can be constructed to equal heights over a square space

rectangular bay: pointed arches (but not round ones) can be constructed to equal heights over rectangular space

buttressing

aisle

narthex

nave

choir, apse, etc.

aisle

buttressing

typical construction of narrow rectangular bays in Gothic cathedral naves and choirs and square bays used in aisles.

Figure 62.   Square and rectangular bays (ribbed vaults).

called a *squinch*. When the dome rests on arches the stone fill is called a *pendentive*. One of the earliest and best examples of a dome on pendentives is found in the Hagia Sophia in what is now Istanbul, Turkey. (Fig. 63).

Another variation of the dome, the *geodesic dome,* relies upon a matrix of tension-compression units in the form of trusses (Fig. 64). These domes require little support and can sit directly on the earth. Because of their intrinsic strength, size and area are not problems for the designers of such domes. One architect has proposed one which would cover the entire New York metropolitan area. Just what the advantages of this huge covering would be are still being debated, but structurally such a dome is apparently feasible. The term *geodesic* seems to be an outgrowth of the philosophy of Buckminster Fuller (a contemporary architect-designer), who maintains that his design principles are based upon the natural linear patterns of the earth and the earth's population.

Arches can also be positioned parallel to each other so that the continuous straight archway produced by the close proximity of round arches form a "tunnel vault" or "barrel vault." Such tunneling requires a substantial buttressing along the sides. Consequently, buildings constructed with this structural base usually have their windows above the "springing," where the walls are not as thick. Romanesque architecture is of this order. Later, the use of intersecting tunnels proved useful by providing more open space in the central arena or nave. The drawings in Fig. 65 demonstrate the essential features of intersecting vaults. Designing in the form of a cross was not entirely symbolic; it also had its functional and material aspects.

When the arch was expanded to include noncircular geometry, differing vault arrangements became possible. With the round arch it was imperative that the base support be of a basic square design, since the apex of the round arch also determines the distance between the supporting walls. When the apex of the arch is raised beyond its circle geometry to an arch which only gradually moved downward, the base support can be and often is rectangular. In the cathedral at Amiens, the vault is rectangular and the arches

Figure 63. Hagia Sophia interior showing dome pendentives. Hagia Sophia Museum, Istanbul, Turkey.

Figure 64. The U.S. Pavilion (Geodesic Dome), 1967 Worlds Fair, Montreal, Canada. Courtesy, Man and His World, Montreal, Canada.

one hundred forty-six

the groin vault: produced by two intersecting
tunnel vaults eliminating additional buttressing

the tunnel vault (barrel vault)
showing arcades and buttresses

Figure 65.   The Tunnel Vault, the Arcade, and the Groin Vault.

are pointed. They intersect at two different angles (see Fig. 66). There are four roof areas ("bays") between the arches in this particular design. To this basic plan were added two additional arches, which were sometimes used as a designing component as well as a supporting or functional component. These "transverse arches" are responsible for redistributing the roof load, thus allowing for smaller or narrower columns of support. The result is more light and more space. Gothic vaults expand the use of space underneath the arches by the clever use of these supporting devices so that unprecedented space is available for functional service. But along with this functional space came new support problems. The very high vaults of the Gothic cathedral require outside support. Such a resolution was not easy to achieve. But when the architect-designers of these huge structures began using the "flying buttress" as a design component, the solution seemed right. The flying buttress differs from the vault buttress in that the former maintains the characteristic of the arch, which gradually transforms tension into compression, and is attached to the main arch at a point just below the springing (at the base of the clerestory windows—see Fig. 67).

Modern Construction Techniques. Domes and vaults were important architectural innovations which continued to be exploited for many centuries. But the demands for innovation and for size and height brought about new possibilities. In the nineteenth and twentieth centuries, iron became a material with structural possibilities. The Eiffel Tower in Paris and the Crystal Palace in London ushered in both the possibility of height and size. The outcome of these architectural firsts, was the familiar "Chicago construction," an iron-grid support which received a "skin" of brick and, later aluminum, glass, or concrete.

Iron construction is based upon the post-and-lintel structural design, since compression is the primary strain and the tension strain is absorbed by the material rather than by graduated transformation. The intrinsic strength of iron and steel girders eliminates to some extent the need for such transformation. On Manhattan island (with a solid schist base) such construction is theoretically

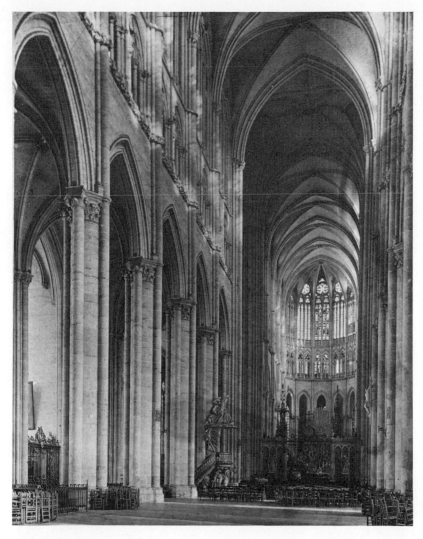

Figure 66. Choir of Notre Dame d'Amiens, showing vaulting. Courtesy Archives Photographiques, Paris.

Figure 67. Notre Dame. Courtesy Caisse Nationale des Monuments Historiques.

one hundred fifty

possible into heights which could only concern the Federal Aeronautics Administration. The current examples of high-rise construction which exploit both interior size and height are the John Hancock Life Insurance Building in Chicago (which stands higher than the Empire State Building Fig. 15) and the World Trade Center towers in New York (which exceed the Chicago building in both size and height Fig. 16).

Like iron, concrete has been used as a building material for centuries, but its use as a structural component was not exploited until this century, when it was discovered that by imbedding iron rods in concrete of heavy aggregates one could develop strength in compression. This "ferroconcrete" or "reinforced concrete" provides the contemporary architect with a combination utilizing the tensile properties of steel and the compressive properties of concrete. Since iron and steel lend themselves nicely to the use of the *truss* (Fig. 68), reinforced concrete often uses a truss of iron to increase its strength. The straining or stressing of the iron rods prior to pouring the concrete aggregate produces a material with a great deal of strength. Such *prestressed concrete* is often used for the flooring sections of bridges and buildings over great spans and as material for cantilevers. The *cantilever* enables the architect to design buildings which are free from exterior support. With them it is possible to maintain continuous windows without structural encumbrances.

The Functional and Decorative Arts

There is a group of arts which have been referred to as the "minor arts"—in part because of their size and transportability, but primarily because they are intended for adornment and function. Some of the main divisions among these arts are weaving, textile designing, ceramics, glass, jewelry, and metalsmithing. Although these arts are historically less monumental and more private than social, they usually carry much of the totemic and social characteristics of the major works. In some cases, miniature sculpture of the

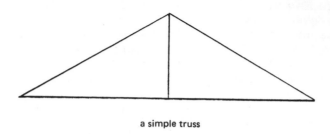

a simple truss

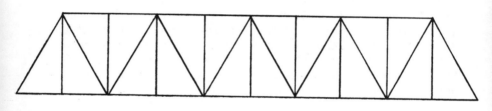

a complex truss

reinforced—concrete beam (ferroconcrete)

Figure 68.   Trusses and reinforced concrete.

same sophistication and interest as the major works of the time were used to adorn everyday objects. In other times, the crafts were essentially the only art forms because of political and social up-heavals. In medieval Europe, as an example, the shifting and mobile nature of many populations precluded the development of any art works except those easily carried and worn. But the crafts do not seem to diminish even when populations become stable, and many times the artists of the day are also the craftsmen. Donatello, a sculptor of the early Renaissance, was a working member of the goldsmithing and stone masonry guilds. Many artists of our time have similarly been engaged in the designing and crafting of func-tional and decorative pieces—e.g., Arp, Brancusi, Matisse, Picasso, and Stuart Davis.

When we view the minor arts, then, we may wish to use the same typology as for the major arts—with some additional consid-erations. Some crafts are functional and consequently limited, and some are simply concerned with ornamentation. Usually one or the other, or both, are evident in the work.

In the past, the designing and execution of clothing, blankets, containers, harnesses, tools, and furniture was an integral part of the industry of each town or village, and the work was done by hand. But in many sections of the world today, handcrafts have either become obsolete or have been turned over to the mass-pro-duction capability of contemporary technology. The limitations placed on the crafts designer in these instances are often in terms of costs; a single designer can often place his designs in hundreds of thousands of homes. Such far-reaching technology coupled with cost consciousness has essentially eliminated much of the func-tional purposes of crafts in America.

In those areas of the world where industrial technology has not yet eliminated the dignity of handcrafts, certain of the tradi-tional processes and materials persist, and even in highly indus-trialized areas there seems to be a reticence to give in to mass production; consequently, several of the crafts flourish where there are no apparent functional reasons for it. The reasons may be more psychological—more related to a need for doing than to a need for the objects themselves.

Ornamentation or decoration is a much more constant focus in the crafts. A well designed *kylix* (an ancient Greek cup made for drinking) probably made its presence welcome beyond its function. It also had the potential for interior decoration—or at least it might seem so to us. Potters today seem to prepare most of their wares for such ornamentation and decoration. Weed pots, pots to hold "dark air," and pots intended for a spot of color and texture are more common to the ceramic crafts today than pots intended for utility. Weaving as produced by the autonomous craftsman today is not so much for wearing as it is for hanging on the walls of homes. This shift in focus seems clear.

Our discussion regarding crafts must include both these traditional functions and purposes of craft objects and the contemporary movement away from utility.

Weaving and Textile Designing. Weaving is accomplished in several ways, but it is always based upon the same basic principles. Plain weaves consist of a group of yarns referred to as a *warp* interlaced with a second group of yarns called the *weft* or *woof*. The weft crosses over and under alternate warp yarns. To allow for this alternation the warp yarns are forced down or up in the loom according to a pattern determined by the weaver. In larger looms this motion is produced by the action of foot levers. Tapestries are basically a plain weave.

In more complicated weaving, additional warps or wefts are used. Brocades, quilts, and coverlets are made by such compound weaving. Figure 69 illustrates the functioning components of a harness loom capable of compound weaving.

Sometimes knotted weaves are used to produce a "pile." The weft in these cases is knotted around the warp, with the ends of the knots protruding from the fabric. By knotting closely and by selecting different colors and values, a "pile" with a design can be produced. Most of the famous rugs from the Near East are produced by this technique, as was the rug by Hans Arp shown in Fig. 70.

Most textile decoration is accomplished by printing appropriate inks and dyes onto the fabric by either stenciling or block-printing techniques. Textile painting, batik and tie dyeing, appliqué and embroidery, though used less than printing, have a long and

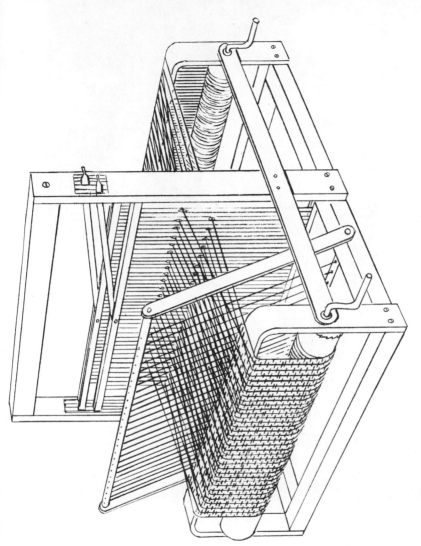

69. Table loom: a two-harness loom is used for plain weaves and various simple pattern techniques. A four, six, or eight harness loom greatly expands the pattern-building possibilities.

Figure 70. Jean (Hans) Arp, *Rug* (1938), wool.
Abby Aldrich Rockefeller Fund; collection, The Museum of Modern Art.

varied history in most cultures. Of these, batik and tie dyeing are perhaps the least known and warrant a brief description here.

Batik is a process which appears to have developed in India and Java from around A.D. 400, and is to this day widely used in those areas for designing silk and cotton. Melted wax painted onto the fabric penetrates in and around the fibers, preventing the dyes from reaching those areas. After dyeing the cloth containing the wax designs, the wax is removed by either heat or chemicals. Subsequent waxings and dyings produce a rich and varied marbled design, especially when the hardened wax is "crackled" by crushing it prior to dipping.

In *tie-dyeing,* gatherings of cloth tied tightly by strings produces intricate and symmetrical designs when dye is applied.

Ceramics and Glass. Ceramics and glass blowing are crafts which have persisted throughout history in both functional and nonfunctional forms. *Ceramics* are produced by heating dried clay objects to a temperature high enough to fuse the platelets or particles of material which comprise the clay body. Low-firing clays may mature at temperatures from 1,400°F to 1,800°F, whereas high-firing clays such as porcelain may require temperatures up to 2,800°F to vitrify.

Neither the processes for forming nor the material being used in the formation of ceramics has changed appreciably since the neolithic potters of Crete and Mesopotamia produced their containers and ceremonial objects. The processes have become less demanding, perhaps, with the use of iron, electricity, and piped fuel, but the procedures themselves remain relatively constant.

To form the clay, the potter may use a rotating wheel and gradually pull the clay into a thin-walled cylindrical shape (see Fig. 71), or he may engage in a sculptural forming process where symmetry gives way to other considerations. Today's potters seem to be forming objects quite removed from function, being more related, perhaps, to ceremonial vessels and decorative objects (see Fig. 72).

Glass is formed by blowing it into molds, open air, or special environments while it is in a thick, fluid state—molten but viscous. A

Figure 71.   David Burton working on a potter's wheel.

Figure 72. Groups of pots by Kenneth Biettel.

one hundred fifty-nine

rhythm of movement between forming and heating allows the craftsman to develop the form over an extended period of time. His tools are of charred hardwood.

Of all the ancient materials, glass provides the most luminous opportunities—from clear transparent images to translucent and nearly opaque luminescence. When light strikes glass it produces refractory images in its immediate environment. This unique quality was unrivaled except in gemstones until the development of plastics in the twentieth century.

Fluxing controlled batches of refined silica with high percentages of lead produces a clear and flawless lead crystal which is suitable for chipping, grinding, and, in its molten state, carving (see Fig. 73).

Jewelry and Metalsmithing. The craft of metal forming and the long history of body adornment has resulted in exquisitely refined tools and processes for the contemporary craftsman. In Fig. 74 an early and sophisticated example of metal forming is shown. To raise surfaces in this fashion, the craftsman must work on a tool which is firm enough to support the metal but soft enough to give way under the repeated hammering required to "move" the metal. Pitch is often used for this purpose. Metal folding, hammer welding, soldering, granulation, enameling, lapidary, engraving, and etching are all both ancient and modern techniques in jewelry making and metal forming.

The jewelry designer must consider the function of his design. If it is a ring, it must not interfere with finger movement or present rough edges to surrounding fingers; if it is a necklace it must conform in some manner with the anatomy of the wearer; and if it is an earring it must not be too heavy for comfort nor too long so as to interfere with its freedom above the shoulder. But beyond such functional limitations, the craftsman is free to explore his own impulses toward a new and personal order in his designing.

Historically, the minor arts have also included working in wood, leather, ivory, jade, and other materials. Furthermore, the makers of tools, weapons, harnesses, carts, furniture, and building

Figure 73. Lead crystal bowl. Collection of Dona Banek Bradley.

Figure 74.   The Vaphio Cups (c. 1500 B.C.).

ornamentation have been integrally involved in the design decisions peculiar to the functional and decorative arts (Fig. 75 and 76).

The availability of material and the life style of individual groups within a society has always dictated to some extent the nature of the crafts they pursued and the processes they used. The tools of the American Indian, for example, were those for the manufacture of small amounts of needed foodstuffs and for weaponry. Their jewelry was made of seeds, kernels, and feathers as often as metal glass, and ceramic. The crafts of tattooing and body painting have also been practiced by both primitive and complex social groups.

The minor arts have been a very important dimension of community and social life, and although their functional purposes have diminished in industrialized societies the ornamental and decorative purposes of these arts has not. And these embellishments—concerns for a dimension beyond survival—appear to be strongly evident in both the environments developed by individuals and the choices made by them among available tools and items of utility.

Figure 75. Carved sign, hardware dealer's (1820.) Mass-Ca-25. Courtesy National Gallery of Art, Index of American Design.

one hundred sixty-four

Figure 76. "Washington Elm" chair. Courtesy the Smithsonian Institution.

THE ARTIST

The view of the artist as a recluse who performs his magic in secret carrels and is "discovered" only after he is dead is true in many cases. But it is also true that many artists throughout the history of art have enjoyed not only recognition but the largesse offered by private, religious, and state patrons during their lives. As a group, artists are probably indistinguishable from any other group in background, education, opportunity, and inclinations. These characteristics which delineate artist from nonartist have little to do with the conventions of race, creed, or politics (there are both right-wing and left-wing artists), but instead with the intensity and drive evident in their needs for the expression of feelings about things.

Many more people practice the arts today than in other times, not only because the arts are more highly disseminated among the general population of the country, but also because the increase in leisure time coupled with a decrease in the need for manual labor has created the climate for involvement in the several arts. But not all who claim the name fit the cast. Those who have other occupations and who often band together in small groups seldom achieve the status afforded those whose lives are absolutely devoted to their art. In times past the artist was easily identified as the one who made art objects. But today, objects are not always viewed as the appropriate criteria. Some art today is simply conceptual and does not result in identifiable objects—only ideas. The distinction between artist and nonartist may have little to do with the making of either objects or ideas. It may refer to a world view and a personal life style based on that view. The only ultimate uniqueness which can be attributed to the artist is, perhaps, his choice and use of a medium of expression, even though certain characteristic approaches to art appear sufficient to warrant our consideration.

A characteristic which can often be observed throughout the long history of art and artists is the propensity toward a new and exaggerated view of traditional subject matter. The serious disagreements between Michelangelo and Pope Julius II had partially to do with the stubbornness and volcanic temper of Michelangelo, but also with his perpetual insistence on autonomy of interpretation. As an example, we may recall that Pope Julius had intended the panels on the ceiling of the Sistine Chapel to contain a series showing the twelve apostles of Christ, but the final result was a quite different iconography based upon Plato's three stages: the world of matter, the world of becoming, and the world of being. Michelangelo included a drunk Noah and pagan sibyls as well as God-fearing prophets in his presentations.

Some fifty years later another Italian painter, Paolo Veronese, was called to account before the Inquisition to defend his inclusion of "dogs, dwarves and German soldiers" in his huge painting originally called *The Last Supper* or *Feast in the House of Simon.* Veronese defended himself by claiming artistic license and pointing to Michelangelo's use of pagans and nudes for the Sistine Chapel. The Inquisition demanded that certain changes be made, but instead Veronese simply changed the name of the work to *Feast in the House of Levi,* thus maintaining the integrity of the work as it was originally conceived.

Beyond the politics of subject matter, artists often exaggerate and change the form of subjects toward a new view or interpretation of events. In a long-established tradition, portraits were often completed of persons in the guise of other persons and gods. Thus Rembrandt often painted his wife, Saskia, as that which she was not in real life—except, perhaps, to him. The combination of human with animal forms, apparitions, and mythological beasts, has also been a dimension of the artist's spirit (especially during romantic periods). The mythological beasts expressed in the art of Persia, China, and medieval Europe, the paintings of Francisco Goya and Pablo Picasso, and juxaposition of life with death and the unknown have all resulted in peculiar and innovative subject matter changes.

A second characteristic sometimes evident in artists' work may be their apparent need to present innovative visual, aural, or tactile expressions of their feelings about social issues. Francisco Goya, as an example, reacted strongly to the selling out of his country (Spain) by an insensitive, retarded, and powerful ruling family to the clever machinations of imperial France. The sellout resulted in street fighting in Madrid in May of 1808 and a series of executions of Spanish patriots on Spanish soil. His feelings were vented in the magnificent painting called "the Executions of May 3, 1808." Goya also produced a series of etchings and aquatints called "The Disasters of War," which were titled with questions such as "To What End?" and included tormenters and victims both dead and alive. This strong and convicted artist was eventually banished from his homeland and died in exile in Bordeau, France, in 1828.

Honoré Daumier, a cartoonist with a strong social commitment, became so involved in his work that he began painting—producing works with messages about the conditions of his time. He painted about the rich, the follies of art galleries, and the plight of the poor. His titles were also indicative of his involvement in the politics and social conditions of his time ("First Class Carriage," "Fourth Class Carriage," "This One May Be Released," "Legislative Paunch"). His productions in many ways foreshadow Bill Mauldin's cartoons of World War II.[6] Like a good newsman, Daumier covered his "beat" with objectivity intensified by personal conviction. But unlike most newsmen, he attempted to express these convictions in a much broader framework than simple newspaper cartoons. There was a sensitivity, beyond the immediate condition, toward the larger issues which brought the condition into being; so he turned to painting.

Pablo Picasso, upon learning of the circumstances surrounding the bombing of Guernica, Spain, in 1937, did his most monumental work. Guernica is a small Basque village in Spain which was politically opposed to the ruling politic. Upon agreement with Franco, German bombers moved over the town and virtually eliminated it. One pilot in referring to his actions over Guernica spoke of the visual effect of the striking bombs as "blossoms opening up," apparently oblivious to the reality of suffering and destruction he was wreaking on the village below.

Picasso's work, *Guernica* (on extended loan to the Museum of Modern Art in New York until it is safe to return it to Spain), describes in a semiabstract way the terror, mutilation, distendedness, and horror of such bestial extensions of man, speaking beyond the Guernica tragedy to the condition itself.

But many artists show no direct interest in either politics or social affairs, and some, like Picasso, are only involved for very short periods of time. At best we can only generalize that this characteristic has been strong in the history of contemporary art, but that it is by no means inclusive. Nor can any claim be made for this characteristic as belonging solely to artists. People in all walks of life have been deeply involved in social and political criticism. The only uniqueness is, perhaps, the manifestations themselves—in objects, movements, sounds, and words.

Artists work toward uniqueness of expression as discussed earlier in this text; they are creative. This characteristic has received some attention among psychologists and others who study the nature of human behavior. But it is a very illusive quality, escaping most attempts at lucid definition. Creative people achieve *flexibility,* or the ability to see second possibilities. They develop *fluency* by operating in many spheres; *originality* by learning to ask uncommon questions—remote, clever, and unusual. They are highly *curious* about the possibilities of new experiences.

Artists have the courage to expose themselves to the possibility of failure, since the establishment of a new form demands freedom from the tyranny of old structures. And this characteristic is different from simple elaboration. It is a reversal of the old order and a reversal of the logic which produced it. Arthur Koestler speaks of such "reversals" as a basis for mythology and the development of plot.

> In the classical tragedy, . . . it is the gods, or the stars who turn the tables on the mortal hero, or lure him into appointments in Samara. They particularly like to use seemingly harmless coincidences—the blind gaps in the meaningful order of events—as levels of destiny. In later forms of literature, it is characters which are made to stand on their heads, or are turned inside out like a glove. Prince Mishkin, the "Idiot," is revealed as a sage in reverse; saints are sinners, sinners are saints, heroes are cowards, adults are children, and every Jekyll has something to Hyde.[7]

And it is no secret that the dualism of object-nonobject as expressed in the figure-ground juxtaposition of the Yang and Yin provide us with a symbol of the constant possibility of the alternate. The creative person may have a greater capacity for ambiguity and a greater willingness to tolerate puzzling and open-ended situations. Sometimes these reversals become manifestos for reform in the arts. Paul Klee, a Swiss artist (who was also an accomplished violinist), anticipated the move toward autonomy and away from conventions by claiming that, for himself, he had to develop his work from specific instances entirely remote from hypotheses. He claimed also that he desired to remove himself from technique—one of the mainstays of the academy. Such a highly individualistic approach could only expand the possibilities for art in the future. The question as to how much of an artist's individual style is merely the product of a social development must be asked when art movements are discussed, since the dual role of artist as reflector and artist as prophet are both evident.

The ways and means of expression change with the times,

and it is often possible to place a work of art into an historical context by studying the color palette, the form distortions, the subject matter, the iconography (use of symbols), and even the size of the work. Artists are products of and participants in the social and cultural milieu of a particular time, and even in their positions of resistance or change they reflect their involvement. In ancient Greece, for example, one of the apparent results of the lowly status assigned to women around 600 B.C. was the size of the sculptures of females called *kourai*—about half life-size, compared to the life-size male statuary. This phenomenon was apparently consistent among all the anonymous Greek sculptors of the time, even though earlier Egyptian work had afforded full status to their queens.

The sixteenth-century Dutch idea that art belongs in homes and not palaces influenced both the size and color of paintings. And this is one important reason why many of the paintings of Vermeer, Hals, and Rembrandt are small, intimate, and subtle in coloring. The full-hued paintings of Tintoretto and the enormous size of some of the paintings of Michelangelo and Rubens were neither appropriate nor acceptable to sixteenth-century art buyers interested in home paintings.

Gothic sculpture as exemplified in the sculptural programs of the Chartres cathedral indicates a social priority on piety, denial, and sacrifice, as opposed to the full-bodied work of Michelangelo and, later, Bernini. In the twentieth century, those who wished to become a part of abstract expressionism accepted a social invitation to do so. Wassily Kandinsky's treatise on the supremacy of abstraction was based already on a cultural drift toward impulsive and unconscious form, and the pressures on artists to align themselves with the "new aesthetic" were strong. When we speak of the art of the first half of the twentieth century we are, therefore, compelled to speak of a particular kind of art, involving particular distortions—culturally distinct from other times.

Within these social styles, however, there is a great deal of room for flexibility, and it is in this flexibility that the individual interpretation of a social concern can happen. Even though the sixteenth-century Dutch painters worked on a small scale and used subtle colors, it is readily possible to identify the unique differences between their individual "styles."

Individual style was once described by George Bernard Shaw as being the result of his early commitment to a form distortion followed by a lifetime of explanation. Apparently, Shaw believed his earliest statement was his only major statement and that all of his writings thereafter were simply elaborations or "explanations" of his early decision. Such a notion would certainly account for individual style, not only in art, but in all human affairs. An expansion of this idea is given by Professor Morse Peckham in his book *Man's Rage for Chaos*,[8] where he denies art as the construction of order but rather a drive toward disorder, and maintains that first examples become *constructs* (defining parameters) within which all subsequent work is done. Thus Peckham's view of art style is that it is the result of a series of explanations ("Explanatory Mode") regarding the first construct ("Exemplary Mode").

Some contemporary writers believe that social "style" is more in keeping with the new demands being made on people by the steadily growing and narrowing values of a monolithic science age. Jack Burnham has suggested that the primary task of the young artist today is to battle against sales. He suggests that he must relinquish his position as both craftsman and entrepreneur if he wishes to participate in the world-at-large. He must become immune to sales by utilizing the most fugitive and ultracommon materials. "By making the unsaleable commercially desireable the artist may shift aesthetic perspective and in this case so radically that nothing is left which is not potentially art."[9]

Should this prognosis come into being, such involvement in the "remaking of society" might become the new "social style" although individual approaches to style will probably remain. The personal distortions of the new social construct will comprise "individual style," as they always have in the past.

This short chapter ends, appropriately, with some sketches and glimpses of the private meanings which bring the arts into being as related by artists themselves:

George Braque (a twentieth-century French painter instrumental in developing cubism) spoke of art to Alexander Liberman:

> The painting materializes in contact with nature. Painting is a meditation. It is contemplation, for the painting is made in the head. ...I do not believe in any one thing. I do not believe in this or this [he touched an object on a small table]. I do not believe in things; I believe only in their relationship, in their circumstances. Circumstances bestow reality on things. In Zen it is said, "Reality is not this, it is the fact of being this." This is a paper knife, but if I use it as a shoehorn, it becomes a shoehorn. For things to exist, there must first come into being a relationship between you and the things, or between the things themselves."

And again:

> The painting is finished when the idea has disappeared. The idea in a painting is like the launching cradle of a ship. It is like the scaffolding used in the building of those enormous ships. After the ship is built, it floats; it has left the cradle useless and forgotten. The idea for a painting is similar. You use the idea to build, to guide, and, when your painting is strong enough, it goes off. It floats; it no longer needs the idea to uphold it. It goes off to lead its own life, as the ship does.[10]

Auguste Rodin, caught up in the controversy surrounding the use of photography as an art, discussed a dimension of art which provides us with his insightful view of the advantage of a time-space factor in art objects:

> If, in fact, in instantaneous photographs, the figures, though taken while moving seem suddenly fixed in mid-air, it is because, all parts of the body being reproduced exactly at the same twentieth or fortieth of a second, there is no progressive development of movement as there is in art.
> ... It is the artist who is truthful and it is photography which lies, for in reality time does not stop, and if the artist succeeds in producing the impression of a movement which takes several moments for accomplishment, his work is much less conventional than the scientific image, where time is abruptly suspended.

one hundred seventy-three

... Gericault is criticized because in his picture "Epsom Races" (Course d'Epsom), which is at the Louvre, he has painted his horses galloping, fully extended, *ventre à terre*, to use a familiar expression, throwing their front feet forward and their back feet backward at the same instant. It is said that the sensitive plate never gives the same effect. And, in fact, in instantaneous photography, when the forelegs of a horse are forward, the hind legs, having by their pause propelled the body onward, have already had time to gather themselves under the body in order to recommence the stride, so that for a moment the four legs are almost gather together in the air, which gives the animal the appearance of jumping off the ground, and of being motionless in this position.

Now I believe that it is Gericault who is right, and not the camera, for his horses *appear* to run; this comes from the fact that the spectator from right to left sees first the hind legs accomplish the effort whence the general impetus results, then the body stretched out, then the forelegs which seek the ground ahead. This is false in reality, as the actions could not be simultaneous; but it is true when the parts are observed successively, and it is this truth alone that matters to us, because it is that which we see and which strikes us.

Note besides that painters and sculptors, when they write different phases of an action in the same figure, do not act from reason or from artifice. They are naively expressing what they feel. Their minds and their hands are as if drawn in the direction of the movement, and they translate the development by instinct. Here, as everywhere in the domain of art, sincerity is the only rule.[11]

Rodin's frequent references to "long action" as opposed to "arrested motion" assisted his arguments against photography—at least of the snapshot variety—as art.

Constantin Brancusi, a twentieth-century sculptor born in Rumania, was described by Liberman as a combination of a Buddist monk and Merlin the magician: a sage mysterious and wise. Brancusi's views on the requirements for being an artist are reflected in the following statement:

I do not follow what is happening in art movements. When one finds his own direction, he is so busy that there is no time.

Why have pupils? One cannot teach soul. For them everything has to be prepared on a conveyor belt. Then one is not free anymore if he feels like doing something. Young artists see things from the outside. They see the surface. One must forget what one learns. . . . To see far is one thing, to get there is something else.[12]

Pablo Picasso in referring to cubism expressed:

I saw that everything had been done. One had to break, to make one's revolution and start at zero. I made myself go toward the new movement. The problem is how to pass, to go around the object and give a plastic expression to the result. The secret of many of my deformations—which many people do not understand—is that there is an interaction, an inter-effect between the lines in a painting; one line attracts the other and at the point of maximum attraction the lines curve in toward the attracting point and form is altered.

This change through attraction, that's what the collector never sees and will never understand in a painting, he added, contemptuously. And often one does a painting really for a corner of the canvas that no one looks at. One does a whole painting for one peach, and people think just the opposite—that the particular peach is but a detail.

Giacometti (a contemporary Italian sculptor) spoke to Liberman of the creative impulse:

No one decides "I'm going to do sculpture," or "I'm going to do painting." One just does it. It's an absurd activity. One does things through mania, obsession, through an automatic need that escapes the understanding.

And again:

I've been fifty thousand times to the Louvre. I have copied everything in drawing, trying to understand. *Art is more what one sees than what one reads*[14] [italics added].

Giacometti was pointing to the primary barrier to experiencing the arts. We cannot appreciate art solely by reading about it or hearing lectures about it. We must actually become willing to encounter art objects first-hand and to stop for a moment to allow our feelings to develop. The more we encounter art objects the more we can be freed from our preconceptions about art—the more we can ignore the typologies which served our earliest needs and the more we can find meaning in the artist's drive toward developing objects, sounds, words, and movements which serve to fill the gaps between our knowing and our feeling.

Figure 77.   Leonard Cave in his Studio. Courtesy William Stukey.

NOTES

1. Read, H., *The Meaning of Art* (Baltimore: Pelican Penguin Books, 1931), pp. 35–36.
2. Lommel, A., *Shamanism: The Beginning of Art* (New York: McGraw-Hill Book Company, 1970), p. 16.
3. Janson, H.W., *History of Art* (Englewood Cliffs: Prentice Hall, Inc., and New York: Harry N. Abrams, Inc., 1962).
4. Birdwhistell, R., *Kinesics and Context* (Philadelphia: University of Pennsylvania Press, 1970).
5. Rodin, A. in *August Rodin* (London: Phaidon Press Ltd., 1965).
6. William Mauldin, *Up Front* (Cleveland and New York: World Publishing Co., 1945, and New York: Norton, 1968).
7. Koestler, Arthur, *The Act of Creation* (New York: The MacMillan Company, 1964), p. 197. Copyright © Arthur Koestler, 1964.
8. Peckham, Morse, *Man's Rage For Chaos* (Philadelphia: Chilton Company, 1965).
9. Burnham, Jack, "Art In The Marcusean Analysis"; Monograph Number 6, *Penn State Papers In Art Education* (University Park, Pa., 1969), p. 19.

10. Georges Braque in Liberman, A., *The Artist In His Studio* (New York: The Viking Press, 1968), pp. 140–41.
11. Auguste Rodin in Holt, E.G., *From The Classicists To The Impressionists* (Garden City: Doubleday-Anchor, 1957–58), p. 409.
12. Constantin Brancusi in Liberman, A., *The Artist In His Studio* (New York: The Viking Press, 1968), p. 171. Copyright in all countries of the International Copyright Union by Alexander Liberman. All rights reserved. Reprinted by permission of The Viking Press, Inc.
13. Pablo Picasso in Liberman, A., *The Artist In His Studio* (New York: The Viking Press, 1968), p. 113.
14. Alberto Giacometti in Liberman, A., *The Artist In His Studio* (New York: The Viking Press, 1968), p. 278.

INDEX

Amiens Cathedral, 36, 144
Aquatint, 122
Appolonius, 44
Arch, Corbeled, 50, 141
Arch, Round, 50, 139, 141, 144
Armature, 91
Arp. H., 51, 153, 154
Atmospheric Perspective, 16

Batik, 157
Bernini, 171
Bistre (bister), 70
Black Chalk, 65
Brancusi, C., 51, 153, 174
Braque, G., 173
Broderson, M., 25, 30

Brueghel, P., 21, 27
Burin, 117
Burnham, J., 172

Capp, A., 8
Cartoon, 55
Carving, 81, 83, 84
Casein, 100
Casting, 91, 93
Ceramics and glass, 157
Chalk, 65
Charcoal, 62, 63
Chicago Construction, 148
Cire Perdue, 94
Collograph, 114
Columbia, Maryland, 136

Conte, N.J., 63, 65
Corbusier, Le', 44, 50, 51
Corinthian, 139
Cromlech, 138

Daguerre, L., 128
Daumier, H., 8, 168
Davis, S., 153
Degas, E., 68, 81, 91
Distemper painting, 98
Dome, 141
Donatello, 153
Doric, 139
Drawing, 54
Drypoint, 116
Durer, A., 105

Eastman, G., 129
Egg Tempera, 101
Eiffel, G., 132
Emulsion, 100
Encaustic, 99, 100
Etching, 105, 119

Ferro-concrete, 151
Figure, 55
Fixative, 63
Form, 55, 57
Fresco, 98, 99
Fresco-secco, 98, 99
Fuller, B., 144

Gaughin, P., 32
Geodesic Dome, 144
Geometric perspective, 16
Gericault, T., 21, 27, 30, 32, 33, 98
Gesture, 55, 57
Giacometti, A., 176
Van Gogh, V., 27, 30, 32, 33, 35, 98
Goya, F. 8, 168

Graphite, 63, 65
Graves, M., 30
Ground, 55

Hals, F., 97
Hartung, H., 32

Incunabula, 104
Inks, 70, 72
Intaglio, 103, 104, 105
Intonaco, 98
Ionic, 139

John Hancock Building, 39, 151
Julius II, 167

Kandinsky, W., 171
Koestler, A., 170
Kourai, 171
Kylix, 154

LeCorbusier, 44, 50, 51
Liberman, A., 173, 174
Linoleum, 109, 114
Lithography, 123
Lommel, A., 8

Magic realism, 16, 17
Maillol, A., 44
Matisse, H., 32, 44, 153
"Medusa", Raft of the, 21, 30, 33
Metal relief, 114
Mezzotint, 117
Michelangelo, 76, 167, 171
Modeling, 76, 91
Monet, C., 33
Moore, H., 39, 44, 46, 51, 72
Mordant, 120

Niemeyer, O., 44, 46

one hundred eighty-one

Niepce, I., 128

Oil paint, 101, 102

Pantheon, 36
Parthenon, 36
Pastel, 68
Peasant Wedding Feast, 21
Peckham, M., 172
Pencil, 63
Pendentive, 144
Photography, 110, 128
Picasso, P., 44, 91, 153, 168, 169, 176
Pisarro, C., 33
Planographics, 103, 104, 109
Plastic painting, 102, 103
Pollack, J., 32
Post and Lintel, 138
Pre-stressed concrete, 151

Raft of the "Medusa," 21, 30, 33
Read, H., 7
Redon, O., 30
Relief, 103, 104, 105
Rembrandt van Rijn, 55, 97
Renaissance, 63
Retroussage, 114
Rodin, A., 44, 46, 50, 51, 72, 76, 81, 91, 174
Rouault, G., 8
Rubens, P., 171

Saarinen, E., 39, 44, 46, 50, 133
Sanguine, 65
Schongauer, M., 105
Senefelder, A., 123
Sepia, 70
Serigraphy, 126
Silverpoint, 68, 70

Sketch, 54, 57, 59
Soldering, 87
Sound Of Flowers, 31
Squeegee, 128
Squinch, 144
Stairway at Auvers, 28, 31
Stencil, 124
Stonehenge, 138
Stress, 50
Study, 54, 57, 59
Style, 15

Talbot, W., 129
Tie-dyeing, 157
Tintoretto, 171
Tobey, M., 32, 35
Tooker, G., 8
Trompe l'oeil, 16
TWA Terminal, 39

Value, 55, 57
Van Der Rohe, M., 44, 46
Van Gogh, V., 27, 31, 32, 33, 35, 98
Vault, 141
Venus of Willendorf, 36
Vermeer, J., 171
Veronese, P., 167
Voussoir, 141

Walking Man, 44, 46
Water-color, 101
Wax crayon, 68
Wedgewood, T., 128
Welding, 87
Wood Engraving, 112
Woodcut, 105, 109, 110, 112
World Trade Center, 39, 151
Wright, F. L., 44, 46
Written Over The Plains, 28